Anonymous

Regulations of the Education Department Respecting Public

and High Schools and Collegiate Institutes in 1885

Anonymous

Regulations of the Education Department Respecting Public and High Schools and Collegiate Institutes in 1885

ISBN/EAN: 9783337306649

Printed in Europe, USA, Canada, Australia, Japan

Cover: Foto ©Paul-Georg Meister /pixelio.de

More available books at **www.hansebooks.com**

REGULATIONS

OF THE

EDUCATION DEPARTMENT

RESPECTING

PUBLIC AND HIGH SCHOOLS

AND

COLLEGIATE INSTITUTES.

1885.

Toronto:
PRINTED BY "GRIP" PRINTING & PUBLISHING CO., FRONT ST.
1885.

REGULATIONS OF THE EDUCATION DEPARTMENT.

CONTENTS.

REGULATIONS

OF THE

EDUCATION DEPARTMENT, ONTARIO.

APPROVED, AUGUST 25TH, 1885.

PUBLIC SCHOOLS.

ACCOMMODATION.

1. By section 40 of the Public Schools Act, 1885, Trustees of rural schools are required to provide adequate accommodation for at least two-thirds of the actual residents between the ages of five and twenty-one years. In the case of cities, towns and incorporated villages, there is no limitation.

School Site.

2. Every school site should be on a well travelled road, as far removed as possible from a swamp or marsh, and so elevated as to admit of easy drainage.

3. The school grounds should be properly levelled and drained, planted with shade trees and enclosed by a substantial fence.

4. There should be a well or other means for procuring water, so placed and guarded as to be perfectly secure against pollution from surface drainage or filth of any kind.

5. The area of the school site should not be less than half an acre in extent, and if the school population of the section exceeds seventy-five the area should be one acre.

6. The water-closets for the sexes should be several feet apart, and under different roofs. Their entrances should be screened from observation.

7. Proper care should be taken to secure cleanliness and to prevent unpleasant and unhealthy odours.

8. Suitable walks should be made from the school-house to the water-closets, so that the closets may be reached with comfort in all kinds of weather.

School-house.

9. The school-house should be placed at least thirty feet from the public highway.

10. Where the school population of the section exceeds one hundred, the school-house should contain two rooms ; where it exceeds one hundred and fifty, three rooms—an additional room being required for each additional fifty pupils.

11. In each room the area should be at least twelve square feet on the floor, and there should be at least two hundred and fifty cubic feet of air space for each pupil.

12. There should be separate entrances with covered porches and suitable cloak-rooms for boys and girls.

13. The heating apparatus should be so placed as to keep a uniform temperature throughout the room, of at least sixty-seven degrees during the whole day.

14. The windows (both sashes) should be adjusted by weights and pulleys and provided with blinds.

15. Care should be taken to arrange for such ventilation as will secure a complete change of atmosphere three times every hour.

School Furniture.

16. The seats and desks should be so arranged that the pupils may sit facing the teacher.   Not more than two pupils should be allowed to sit at one desk, but single-seated desks are preferred.

17. The height of the seats should be so graduated that pupils of different sizes may be seated with their feet resting firmly upon the floor. The backs should slope backwards two or three inches from the perpendicular.

18. The seats and desks should be fastened to the floor in rows, with aisles of suitable width between the rows ; passages, at least three feet wide, should be left between the outside rows and the side and the rear walls of the room, and a space, from three to five feet wide, between the teacher's platform and the front desks.

19. Each desk should be so placed that its front edge may project slightly over the edge of the seat behind it.   The desk should be provided with a shelf for pupils' books, and the seat should slope a little towards the back.

20. A sufficient number of seats and desks should be provided for the accommodation of all the pupils ordinarily in attendance at the school. There should be at least two ordinary chairs in addition to the teacher's chair.

21. The desks should be of three different sizes. The following dimensions are recommended :—

AGE OF PUPILS.	CHAIRS OR SEATS.			DESKS.			
	Height.		Slope of Back.	Length.		Width.	Height next Pupil.
	Front.	Rear.		Double.	Single.		
Five to Eight years............	12 in.	11½ in.	2 in.	36 in.	18 in.	12 in.	22 in.
Eight to Ten years	13 "	12½ "	2 "	36 "	18 "	12 "	23 "
Ten to Thirteen years	14 "	13½ "	2½ "	36 "	20 "	13 "	24 "
Thirteen to Sixteen years	16 "	15½ "	3 "	40 "	22 "	13 "	26 "

Blackboard, Globes and Maps.

22. There should be one blackboard at least four feet wide, extending across the whole room in rear of the teacher's desk, with its lower edge not more than two and a half feet above the floor or platform, and, when possible, there should be an additional blackboard on each side of the room. At the lower edge of each blackboard there should be a shelf or trough five inches wide for holding crayons and brushes.

The following directions for making a blackboard may be found useful :—
(*a*) If the walls are brick the plaster should be laid upon the brick and not upon the laths as elsewhere ; if frame, the part to be used for a blackboard should be lined with boards, and the laths for holding the plaster nailed firmly on the boards.
(*b*) The plaster for the blackboard should be composed largely of plaster of Paris.
(*c*) Before and after having received the first coat of color it should be thoroughly polished with fine sand paper.
(*d*) The coloring matter should be laid on with a wide, flat varnish brush.
(*e*) The liquid coloring should be made as follows :—Dissolve gum shellac in alcohol, four ounces to the quart ; the alcohol should be 95 per cent. strong ; the dissolving process will require at least twelve hours. Fine emery flour with enough chrome green or lampblack to give color, should then be added until the mixture has the consistency of thin paint. It may then be applied, in long, even strokes, up and down the liquid being kept constantly stirred.

23. Every school should have at least (*a*) one globe not less than nine inches in diameter, properly mounted ; (*b*) a map of Canada ; (*c*) a map of Ontario ; (*d*) maps of the World and of the different Continents ; (*e*) one or more sets of Tablet lessons of Part I. of the First Reader ; (*f*) a standard Dictionary and Gazetteer ; (*g*) a numeral frame ; and a suitable supply of crayons and blackboard brushes.

PROGRAMME OF STUDIES.

24. The programme of studies herein prescribed shall be followed by the teacher as far as the circumstances of his school permit. Any modifications deemed necessary should be made only with the concurrence of the Inspector and the Trustees. In French and German Schools the authorized Readers shall be used in addition to any text books in either of the languages aforesaid.

PROGRAMME OF STUDIES FOR PUBLIC SCHOOLS.

SUBJECT.	1ST CLASS.	2ND CLASS.	3RD CLASS.	4TH CLASS.
READING AND LITERATURE—	Tablet lessons and First Reader.	Second Reader.	Third Reader.	Fourth Reader.
SPELLING, ORTHOGRAPHY, AND ORTHOEPY—	Spelling from reading lessons, on slates and orally.	Spelling from reading lessons, on slates and orally.	Spelling, with verbal distinctions, on copies, and orally.	Systematic orthography and orthoëpy.
WRITING—	Writing on slates and paper.	Writing on slates and paper.	Copy writing. Business forms.	Business forms & accounts.
ARITHMETIC—	Numeration and notation to 1,000; addition and subtraction; mental arithmetic.	Numeration and notation to 1,000,000; multiplication and division; mental arithmetic.	Greatest common measure and least common multiple. Elementary reduction. Compound rules. Mental Arithmetic.	Vulgar and decimal fractions. Elementary percentage and interest. Mental arithmetic.
DRAWING—	The drawing exercises in parts I. and II. First Reader.	Drawing-book No. 1, authorized series.	Drawing-books Nos. 2 and 3.	Drawing-books Nos. 4 and 5.
GEOGRAPHY—	Conversations concerning the earth.	Local geography and elementary definitions. Map of the world.	Definitions. Simple map geography. N. America and Ontario. Map drawing.	Geography of the Continents, Canada and Ontario. Map drawing.
MUSIC—	Rote singing.	Rote singing. Elements of *Musical Notation.*	Simple songs. Elementary ideas of written music.	Song singing. Sacred music. Musical notation.
GRAMMAR AND COMPOSITION—	Oral exercises in language.	Oral and written exercises in language.	Classes of words and their inflections. Simple descriptive writing.	Elements of formal Grammar and Composition.
HISTORY—			History, English and Canadian.	Leading features of English and Canadian History.
OBJECT LESSONS—	Form, size, colour, weight, common objects (parts and qualities).	Subjects of Class I. continued.	Common objects (source, manufacture, uses, etc.). Animals, birds, plants.	
TEMPERANCE, HYGIENE, DRILL (with Calisthenics for Girls), AND MORAL CULTURE—		See details below.		

every day in the school term in which his name is so entered; (2) to be neat and cleanly in his person and habits; (3) to be diligent, truthful, honest, kind, courteous, respectful, and obedient; (4) to conform to all the rules of the school.

26. Any pupil not present at the time prescribed for opening the school may be required to furnish forthwith a written excuse from his parent or guardian, or be denied admittance to the school for the day or half-day, at the discretion of the Principal.

27. Any pupil absenting himself from school, except on account of sickness, shall forfeit his standing in his class, or shall be liable to such other punishment as the teacher may lawfully inflict.

28. No pupil shall be allowed to leave school before the hour appointed for closing, except in case of sickness, or on the request, either oral or written, of the parent or guardian.

29. Any pupil, once admitted to school and duly registered, shall attend at the commencement of each term and continue in attendance regularly until its close, or until he is withdrawn by notice to the teacher to that effect; and any pupil violating this rule shall not be entitled to continue in such school, or be admitted to any other, until such violation is certified by the parent or guardian to have been necessary and unavoidable.

30. Any pupil guilty of any of the following offences, viz.:—(a) persistent truancy; (b) violent opposition to authority; (c) the repetition of any offence after being warned; (d) habitual and wilful neglect of duty; (e) the use of profane or improper language; (f) general bad conduct, injurious to the moral tone of the school; (g) cutting, marring, destroying or defacing any part of the school property; (h) writing any obscene words on the fences, water-closets, or any part of the school premises, may be suspended by the teacher for one month, or until such suspension is removed by assurance of better conduct, or by order of the Trustees.

31. Whenever any teacher suspends a pupil for any of the causes herein named, he shall at once notify the parents or guardians, and the Trustees thereof, stating the reasons for such suspension.

32. The parent or guardian of any pupil suspended may appeal to the Trustees against the action of the teacher, and the decision of the Trustees, or of a majority of them, shall be final.

33. Any pupil who shall be adjudged so refractory by the Trustees or by a majority of them, and by the teacher, that his presence in the school is deemed injurious to the other pupils, may be expelled, and no such pupil shall be readmitted to any school without the written consent of the Public School Inspector.

34. Pupils in cities, towns and villages shall attend such school or department as may be designated by the Trustees, and no transfer from one school or department to another shall be allowed without the consent of the Trustees and the Inspector.

35. No pupil who is affected with or exposed to any contagious disease, shall be permitted to attend school until he produces the certificate of a medical man that all danger from his mingling with the other pupils, or from his exposure to the disease, has passed away.

36. Any pupil absenting himself from an examination, or from any portion thereof, without permission of the teacher, shall not be admitted to any public school, except by authority of the Inspector, in writing; and the names of all such pupils shall be immediately reported by the teacher to their parents and the Trustees.

37. Pupils shall be responsible to the teacher for their conduct on the school premises, or in going to or returning from school, except when accompanied by their parents or guardians, or by some person appointed by them, or on their behalf.

38. No pupil shall be allowed to remain in school unless he is furnished with the books and requisites to be used by him in school, but it shall be lawful for the Trustees to supply him with such books and requisites.

39. No pupil shall have the right to attend school unless, and until, he has paid all the fees imposed by the Trustees for the current month or quarter, as the case may be, and for such books, stationery and other supplies as are authorized under the Public Schools Act.

40. Any school property or furniture injured or destroyed by a pupil, must be made good forthwith by the parent or guardian, under penalty of the suspension of the delinquent.

41. Every pupil entitled thereto shall, when he leaves or removes from a school, receive a certificate of good conduct and standing.

School Hours.

42. The school hours shall be from nine o'clock in the forenoon till four o'clock in the afternoon, unless the trustees by resolution prescribe a shorter period.

43. There shall be a recess of not less than ten minutes each forenoon and afternoon, and at least one hour shall be allowed for recreation during the middle of the school day.

DUTIES OF TEACHERS.

44. In every Public School in which more teachers than one are employed the head teacher shall be called the Principal and the other teachers Assistants.

45. The Principal shall prescribe (with the concurrence of the trustees) the duties of the Assistants, and shall be responsible for the organization, classification and discipline of the whole school.

46. It shall be the duty of every teacher in a Public School—

(1) To see that the school-house is ready for the reception of pupils at least fifteen minutes before the time prescribed for opening the school in the morning, and five minutes before the time for opening in the afternoon.

(2) To classify his pupils strictly according to the programme of studies prescribed by the Education Department, and to make no departure from such classification without the consent of the Trustees and the Inspector.

(3) To prepare a time-table to be posted in some conspicuous part of the room for the guidance of himself and pupils.

(4) To teach diligently and earnestly, according to the most approved methods, the various subjects set forth in the programme of studies prescribed from time to time by the Education Department.

(5) To prevent the use by the pupils of unauthorized text-books.

(6) To make at the end of each school term or at such other time as may be approved by the Inspector, and subject to revision by him, such promotions from one class to another as he may deem expedient.

(7) To practise such discipline in his school as would be exercised by a kind, firm, and judicious parent; to reprove with tenderness and becoming deliberation; to aim at governing his pupils through their affections and reason rather than by force; to encourage them to cultivate kindly and affectionate feelings towards one another, respect for one another's rights, politeness in and out of school, honesty, truthfulness, the practice of correct habits and obedience to all persons in authority over them; and to discountenance quarrelling, cruelty to animals, and the use of profane and improper language.

(8) To give strict attention to the proper ventilation and cleanliness of the school-house; to make and enforce such rules as will ensure the keeping of the school grounds and outbuildings in a neat and cleanly condition.

(9) To see that the school grounds, sheds, and water-closets are kept in proper order; that no damage is done to the furniture, fences, outbuildings, or other school property; to give notice in writing to the Trustees of any necessary repairs or supplies.

(10) To employ (unless otherwise provided for), at such compensation as may be fixed by the Trustees, a suitable person to make fires, sweep the rooms, dust the walls, seats, desks, and other furniture; but no assistant teacher or pupil shall be required to perform such duty unless regularly employed for that purpose as herein provided.

(11) To act as librarian of the school and keep such a record of the books as is prescribed by the regulations respecting libraries.

(12) To keep in the prescribed form a register of the daily attendance of the pupils

(13) To make up all returns to the Inspector or the Education Department, as far as the information required can be supplied from the school register.

(14) To keep the visitors' book, and allow visitors free access to the same.

(15) To attend regularly the Teachers' Institutes held in his county, and to contribute from his experience and observation to their general usefulness.

(16) To give immediate notice to the Trustees of his absence from school through illness or other unavoidable cause.

Collections—Presents—Lost Time.

47. In no school shall collections be taken up or subscriptions received from the pupils, nor shall any bills or other advertisements be distributed by the teacher for any purpose whatever without the consent of the Trustees.

48. Except when severing his connection with the school, no teacher shall receive any presents from the pupils, nor shall he give any medal or prize to any pupil without the consent of the Trustees.

49. No teacher shall make up lost time by teaching on a holiday or during vacations, and any attendance during such time shall be disallowed by the Inspector.

INSPECTORS.

Qualifications.

50. Any person holding either (a) a first-class Provincial certificate, grade A, obtained at the Departmental Examinations, or (b) a degree in arts from any University in Ontario, with first-class honors in one or more of the recognized departments of examination in such University, and furnishing evidence of having taught successfully for five years, (of which at least three years must have been spent in a Public School) shall be eligible to be appointed a Public School Inspector.

County Inspector's Duties.

51. It shall be the duty of every County Inspector—

(1) *To visit each school* under his jurisdiction at least once in each term.

(2) *To spend half a day in each school.* Where a school has several departments, the Inspector should devote half a day to each department. When, however, from the character of the work done, an

Inspector thinks it would be in the interests of the school to extend his visit over the whole day, he should do so. The half day limit is the average time required for each visit.

(3) *To satisfy himself as to the progress made by the pupils from time to time.* This cannot be done without many memoranda of the standing of each class. It will therefore be necessary for the Inspector to make copious notes in regard to each recitation, showing the condition of each class and the proficiency attained in the several subjects of the curriculum. This part of the work should be thorough and searching; and the conclusions arrived at should be based on the Inspector's own observation.

(4) *To examine into the methods of instruction pursued by the teacher.* To do this the Inspector should require the teacher of the school to teach several lessons in his presence. In this way the teacher's methods could be observed and hints given for improvement should he evince any faults of method or of manner. Great attention should be paid to methods: the proper and logical presentation of a subject is so important that success is impossible without it.

(5) *To teach a few model lessons himself.* The proper method of teaching subjects that are found to be neglected or badly taught by the teacher should be exemplified by the Inspector. Here all the qualities which go to form the model teacher should be exercised. His methods of questioning and of receiving answers, of rousing the enthusiasm of the class, of securing attention, of reaching by apt illustration the judgment of the pupils, are all eagerly watched by the teacher and should serve both as a model and as a stimulus to him in the future.

(6) *To ascertain the nature of the discipline exercised by the teacher.* This no doubt will appear from the attention and diligence of the pupils, without special enquiry. The *manner* of the teacher will very soon indicate the nature of the discipline. It would be well, nevertheless, to ascertain whether corporal punishment is frequently resorted to, and if not, what are the punishments (if any) usually inflicted.

(7) *To examine the registers, maps, seats,* and all the internal and external equipments of the school-house (a) registers: he should see that the register is properly and neatly kept, and ascertain whether or not entries are made therein daily; (b) that the maps are suitable and well preserved ; (c) that blackboards are in proper repair, and that crayons and brushes are fully supplied ; (d) that the furniture is generally adequate; that proper attention is paid to the heating (e) and ventilation of the rooms ; (f) that the fences and out-houses are in proper repair; (g) that the School Library is suitably cared for.

(8) *To report to Trustees in regard to such matters as require their attention.* This duty the Inspector should never neglect. The Trustees of a school expect to be informed and directed as to many matters coming under the cognizance of the Inspector, who is, in a certain sense, their

2

officer, and is appointed for the very purpose of aiding them in the discharge of their duties His report, therefore, on the school should be full. Everything coming within the scope of the duties of the Trustees should be mentioned in detail, and in no case should the school grant be withheld, until they have had an opportunity of removing any defect to which their attention has been called.

(9) *To give such advice to teachers as may be deemed necessary.* This part of the Inspector's duty should be performed with tact and delicacy, and perfect frankness. Whatever defects in the teacher's manner, or in his discipline of the pupils, or methods of instruction are discovered during the inspection of the school, should be plainly pointed out. Wherever the Inspector has reason to believe that there is any defect in the organization of the school, or in its classification, or in attention on the part of the pupils, it should be referred to, and the proper remedy suggested. This, of course, should be done privately—not in the presence of the pupils.

(10) *To see that no unauthorized text-books are used in the school.* No books should be placed in the hands of the pupils, except those authorized for their use. Under the disguise of recommending certain works for "home study," many unauthorized text-books are introduced into the school. This should be prevented by the Inspector in the exercise of his authority as an officer of the Education Department.

(11) *To withhold the school grant in certain cases.* Before the school grant is withheld two things are necessary. (1) An opportunity should be afforded the Trustees to remedy the wrong complained of. (2) A full statement of the case should be sent to the Department, and the consent of the Minister of Education obtained. As the grant can be withheld for any violation of the School Act or Departmental Regulations, the power thus conferred should be exercised judiciously, and only when other remedies fail.

(12) *To divide the school grants.* Care should be taken to see that the semi-annual returns of the Trustees are properly added up, and if any doubt exists as to their accuracy they should be compared with the school register. When the division of the grant is made, as required by law, it will be sufficient for the Inspector to send a statement to the Township Treasurer of the amount due each school section, and at the same time to notify the Secretary-Treasurer of each Board of Trustees of the amount due their section. The Trustees can then give an order either to the teacher or to some other person to whom they desire to have the money paid, and on this order the Township Treasurer is authorized to pay the money.

(13) *To decide complaints made within twenty days* in regard to the election of Trustees and other matters. In discharging this duty the Inspector should remember that he is exercising judicial functions and should accordingly proceed with due deliberation. He has a right to withhold his decision until such evidence is produced as he may deem necessary in regard to the question at issue.

(14) *To grant, on examination, temporary certificates.* These certificates should only be granted (1) when petitioned for by a Board of Trustees, and only for the school over which such Board has jurisdiction; and (2) until the date of the next ensuing Departmental Examination; and (3) when it appears that a teacher holding a regular certificate is not available. The consent of the Minister is also necessary in every case.

(15) *To suspend a certificate* when he is fully satisfied that the teacher is incompetent or immoral, or has wilfully violated the school law or the regulations of the Education Department. In the final investigation by which such suspension is to be confirmed or set aside, the fullest opportunity should be afforded the teacher to vindicate himself. Judicial fairness should in this instance also characterize the conduct of the Inspector.

(16) *To visit the County Model School* at least twice in each term. It is very desirable that the Inspector should be present at the opening of the Model School and assist the Principal in its organization. He should also visit the school at least once during the term, and by his presence and counsel encourage the teachers in training in the pursuit of their studies.

City Inspectors.

52. The Inspector of every city or town shall, as far as circumstances admit, be governed by the regulations respecting County Inspectors, and shall, in addition thereto, perform such other duties as may be imposed upon him by the Board of Trustees.

Powers of Inspector.

53. The Inspector, while officially visiting a school, has supreme authority in the school, and has the right to direct teachers and pupils in regard to any or all of the exercises of the school-room. He may either examine the classes himself or direct the teacher to do so. He is at liberty to give such advice to pupils or to the teacher as he may deem necessary. All his counsels, however, should be given in a spirit of kindness, and his authority should be exercised, not with a view to over-awe or intimidate, but to reform abuses, correct mistakes, and inspire confidence and respect. He should be courteous and considerate, and when reproof is necessary it should be tempered with gentleness and sympathy.

HIGH SCHOOLS.

Conditions of Establishment.

54. Any County Council may by resolution recommend the establishment of one or more High schools within its jurisdiction, but such resolution shall take effect only when approved by the Education Department. In asking the concurrence of the Department, parties interested should furnish the Minister of Education with a statement, showing :—

(1) A certified copy of the resolution adopted by the County Council.

(2) The distances of the proposed High school from the nearest existing High schools.

(3) The population of the town or village municipality in which it is proposed to establish the High school.

(4) The value of taxable property in the High school district.

(5) The description of the proposed High school building, as regards—

(a) Its situation; the extent of its site; size of play-ground; and extent of outside conveniences, etc.

(b) A simple plan of the building shewing the number of class-rooms; rooms for teacher; hat, cloak, map and book presses, etc.

55. A written guarantee must be given to the Department by the corporation in which the proposed High school is to be established:—

(1) That a suitable building distinct from the Public school house will be provided ;

(2) That at least two competent teachers will be employed in the proposed High school ;

(3) That all sums necessary for the efficient support of such High school, not provided by the Legislative and county grants, will be raised by local assessment ;

(4) That the expenses incurred by the Education Department in making the necessary inspection for the purpose of reporting to the Minister of Education will be paid.

56. On receipt of this statement and the report of the High school Inspector to whom the matter may have been referred, the Minister of Education will make such recommendations to the Lieutenant-Governor as he may deem expedient.

Accommodation.

57. In order to be entitled to any portion of the grant voted by the Legislature for High School purposes, the Trustees of every High School shall provide the following :—

(a) A site of at least half an acre in extent, well fenced, well drained, planted with shade trees, and suitably provided with walks in front and rear.

(b) A playground, and all other necessary provision for physical exercise.

(c) A well, or other means for supplying pure drinking water.

(d) Separate water closets for the sexes, properly screened from observation.

(e) A building large enough to provide ample accommodation for every pupil in attendance, with all necessary provision for light, heat, and ventilation, and two entrances with covered porches.

(*f*) Suitable separate cloak-rooms for boys and girls, furniture, desks, maps, apparatus, black-boards and Library of reference.

(*g*) A Headmaster, and at least one assistant.

58. In case the High School Inspectors report that the equipment of any High School is insufficient, or that the grounds are too limited in area, or that the school building is inadequate for the accommodation of the pupils, or that the staff or any member thereof is incompetent, the Minister of Education will forthwith notify the Chairman of the Board of Trustees, and on the neglect or refusal of the said Board to comply with the regulations herein contained within a reasonable time, then such High School shall forfeit all claims upon the legislative grant until such time as the regulations are complied with.

COLLEGIATE INSTITUTES.

59. Before any High school can be raised to the status of a Collegiate Institute, the Trustees thereof shall furnish the Minister of Education with a statement, showing :—

(1) The name and literary standing of each master employed, and the subject or subjects of the High school curriculum which he is specially appointed to teach.

(2) The names of the assistants and other teachers occasionally employed, the nature of their duties and the number of their teaching hours per day.

(3) The number of pupils on the school register for each of the two terms next preceding the date of application.

(4) The value of the school property devoted to High school purposes.

(5) The amount expended the previous year in teachers' salaries and maintenance of the school respectively.

(6) The area of the High school site and a simple plan of the building, showing the number of rooms available for school purposes.

(7) A list of the apparatus used in the laboratory, and the cost of the same, the number and names of the maps and the number and names of volumes in the library, and the amount expended for library purposes.

(8) The size and equipments of the gymnasium, and the extent of the outside conveniences.

60. No High School shall hereafter be raised to the status of a Collegiate Institute without such a minimum equipment in the way of library, scientific apparatus, gymnasium, maps, charts and globes, as the maximum required for three or more master schools (not institutes) under regulation 112.

61. Any Collegiate Institute that fails to comply with the conditions prescribed herein for the status of a Collegiate Institute may, on the joint report of the High School Inspectors, be reduced to the rank of a High School, or deprived of the usual legislative grant, at the discretion of the Minister of Education.

ENTRANCE EXAMINATIONS TO HIGH SCHOOLS.

Where Held—Notice to Inspector.

62. At every High School and Collegiate Institute, and at such other places as may be approved by the Minister of Education, there shall be a semi-annual examination for the admission of pupils to High Schools and Collegiate Institutes, in the subjects prescribed for the 4th class of Public Schools, excepting Music and Business forms and Book-keeping.

63. Persons proposing to write at a town or city forming a separate inspectoral division must notify the Inspector of such town or city. In all other cases notice must be sent to the County Inspector, and if more examinations than one are held in the County, the place at which the candidate proposes to write should be named.

64. Applications shall not be received by any Inspector later than the 1st day of June for the summer examination, nor later than the 1st day of December for the winter examination. Where a fee is imposed by the Board of Examiners, all applications must be accompanied by the amount of such fee.

65. The Inspector shall notify the Department not later than the 3rd day of June or the 3rd day of December (as the case may be) in each year, of the number of persons proposing to write at any High sch ol or other place within his jurisdiction.

Presiding Examiner.

66. In cities or towns forming a separate inspectoral division, the Inspector of such city or town shall conduct the examination, and, in conjunction with the Board of Examiners for such city or town, shall read the papers and report to the Department.

67. In counties in which more High schools than one are situated, the Inspector for the county shall elect at which High school he will preside, and shall notify the Department of the choice he makes. In each of the other High schools the Principal of the High school shall preside.

68. In the case of examinations being held where there is no High school, the Inspector shall appoint a presiding Examiner, notice of which appointment shall be sent to the Department ; but all such examinations shall be considered as held in affiliation with a High School to be named in such notice, and the Inspector within whose jurisdiction such examination is held shall be a member of the Board of Examiners.

69. Where, from the number of candidates or any other cause, additional presiding Examiners are required, the Inspector shall make such appointments as are necessary, but no person shall be eligible to be appointed presiding Examiner who has any pupils writing for admission at a High school where he is presiding.

70. Where more examinations than one are held in an Inspectoral division the papers will be sent by the Education Department to the Inspector, who shall be responsible for their delivery to the various presiding Examiners within his jurisdiction.

71. The parcel containing the examination papers shall not be opened till the morning of the examination day, nor shall any envelope containing the papers in any subject be opened until the time appointed in the time-table for the examination in such subject.

Duties of Examiners.

72. The presiding Examiner shall be in attendance at the place appointed for the examination at least fifteen minutes before the time fixed for the first subject, and shall see that the candidates are supplied with the necessary stationery, and seated so far apart as to afford reasonable security against copying.

73. He shall open the envelope containing the papers in each subject in full view of the candidates at the time prescribed, and shall place one paper on each candidate's desk.

74. He shall exercise proper vigilance over the candidates to prevent copying, and shall allow no candidate to communicate with another, nor permit any person, except a co-examiner, to enter the room during the examination.

75. He shall see that the candidates cease writing promptly at the proper time, fold and endorse their papers properly, and in every respect comply with the regulations herein contained.

Duties of Candidates.

76. Every candidate shall be in attendance at least fifteen minutes before the time fixed at which the examination is to begin, and shall occupy the seat allotted by the presiding Examiner. Any candidate desiring to move from his allotted place or to leave the room, shall first obtain permission from the presiding Examiner to do so. Any candidate leaving shall not return during the examination in the subject then in hand.

77. Every candidate shall write his answers on one side only of the paper and shall number each answer. He shall arrange the sheets numerically, according to the questions, and fold them once crosswise, endorsing them with his name, the name of the subject, and the name of the place at which he is examined. No paper shall be returned to a candidate after being placed in the hands of the Examiner.

78. Any candidate who is found copying from another or allowing another to copy from him, or who brings into the examination room any book, note, or paper having any reference to the subject on which he is writing, shall be required by the presiding Examiner to leave the room, and his papers, and the papers of all parties concerned, shall be cancelled.

79. Candidates for examination in Drawing must place their drawing books in the hands of the presiding Examiner on the morning of the first day of the examination. Every exercise must be certified by the teacher as being the candidate's own work, and should shew his progress during, at least, three months. Examiners should inspect the books, and return them to the candidates on the evening of the second day.

Reading and Valuing Papers.

80. At the close of the examination the presiding Examiner shall submit the answers of the candidates to the Board of Examiners, whose duty it shall be to make such arrangements as may be deemed most convenient for reading and valuing the same, and for reporting the results to the Education Department.

81. The papers of the different candidates shall, in order to secure uniformity in valuation, be so distributed, that the same Examiner shall read and value the answers in the same subject throughout.

Marks to be Assigned.

82. In reading the papers the Examiners shall be guided by the following schedule of values :—

Reading, 50 marks ; Drawing, 50 ; Neatness, 35 ; Writing, 20 ; Orthography and Orthoëpy, 50 ; Literature, 100 ; Arithmetic, 100 ; Grammar, 100 ; Geography, 75 ; Composition, 100 ; History, 75.

83. The marks for Neatness shall be divided equally among the last seven subjects, and shall be added to the values herein assigned to those subjects. Of the marks for Drawing, 25 will be assigned to the paper on that subject, and a maximum of 25 may be awarded as the result of the inspection of the candidate's drawing book. In examining Reading, special attention should be paid to Pronunciation, Emphasis, Inflection and Pause. One mark shall be deducted for each misspelt word wherever it occurs.

84. In every case, the marks shall be distinctly written on the face of each answer. The special marks for Neatness and the marks to be deducted for bad spelling are to be distinctly and separately marked on the candidates' papers in which such marks are allowable.

85. Any candidate who obtains one-third of the marks in each subject (neatness included), and one half of the aggregate may be admitted to a High School by the Board of Examiners, subject to the approval of the Education Department. On receipt of such approval the Board of Examiners shall issue a certificate of admission to each successful candidate.

86. In the case of candidates who fail in reaching the standard above prescribed, but who, in the opinion of the Board of Examiners, should be recommended to the favourable consideration of the Education Department, the Report of the Board should show on what special grounds such recommendation is based.

87. The report of the Examiners, shewing the marks awarded and by whom each set of the papers was read, together with the answers of the candidates, shall be transmitted by the Inspector to the Education Department (charges prepaid) within ten days after the close of the examination.

88. Any candidate may, within one month after the result of the examination has been announced, appeal to the Education Department for a re-reading of his examination papers, providing the grounds of such appeal are specifically stated, and the sum of two dollars deposited with the Department.

Fees of Examiners.

89. Every Examiner presiding or reading and valuing papers shall be entitled to be paid the sum of four dollars for each day during which he is so engaged. Where, however, the County Council agrees to pay the sum of seventy-five cents per candidate, the Board of Examiners shall by resolution determine what sum shall be paid each Examiner.

90. All accounts for stationery, express charges, postage, attendance, presiding, reading and valuing papers, or for any other purpose connected with the examination, shall be certified by at least one Inspector, and shall be forthwith paid as provided in section 42 of the High Schools Act.

91. The Board of Examiners for each High School may at its discretion require each candidate to pay a fee not exceeding one dollar.

School Hours in High Schools.

92. Every High School and Collegiate Institute shall open each school day not later than nine o'clock in the forenoon, and shall close not later than four o'clock in the afternoon. Such intervals for recreation during the day shall be allowed as the Trustees may deem expedient.

Courses of Study.

93. Pupils, on entering the High School, shall pursue one or other of the following Courses :—(a) That prescribed for a High School Commercial

Course. (*b*) That prescribed for Matriculation into any of the Universities of Ontario, or for the Preliminary Examination of any of the learned professions. (*c*) That prescribed for a Teacher's Non-professional Certificate. Special Classes for the study of Agricultural Chemistry may be established by the Trustees, with the concurrence of the Head Master.

94. Any High School pupil may take, in addition to the subjects in the course selected, such subjects in any of the other courses as may be agreed upon by his parent or guardian and the Head Master of the High School; but no subject not mentioned in the High School Course of Study shall be taken up by any pupil without the consent of the Education Department.

95. In classifying his pupils, the Head Master shall be guided by the capabilities of his pupils and the circumstances of the school. The Head Master is not restricted in the sub-division of Forms, but he shall make at least two sub-divisions in Form I.

96. It shall be the duty of the Head Master to prescribe the number of pupils in each Form, the division of subjects among his assistants, and the order in which each subject shall be taken up by the pupils—whether or not all the subjects in the Course of Study shall be taught concurrently; also, to make such promotions from one Form to another as he may deem expedient; and generally so to limit the sub-divisions of each Form as will best promote the interests of his pupils.

97. In every High School and Collegiate Institute, Vocal Music should be taught, as well as the theory thereof; Chemistry and Physics should be taught experimentally, and Botany practically; and it shall be the duty of the High School Inspectors to report specially those schools in which this recommendation is not observed. Gymnastics, Drill and Calisthenics shall also form part of the obligatory course.

98. The following subjects, as herein limited, shall constitute the Course of Study in the different Forms:—

Form I.

1. *Reading (oral) and Principles of.*—A general knowledge of the principles of elocution; reading with proper expression, emphasis, inflection, and force.

2. *Orthography and Orthoëpy.*—The pronunciation, the syllabication, and the spelling from dictation, of passages from any English author, and the spelling of all non-technical English words.

3. *English Grammar.*—Etymology and Syntax; exercises.

4. *Composition.*—The framing of sentences and paragraphs; familiar and business letters; paraphrasing; synonyms; correction of errors; themes based on the prose literature prescribed for this Form.

5. *Literature.*—The critical reading of such works as may be prescribed by the Education Department from time to time.

6. *History.*—The leading events of Canadian and English History.

7. *Geography.*—Political, physical, and mathematical Geography. Map Geography generally; Canada and the British Empire more particularly.

8. *Arithmetic and Mensuration.*—Arithmetic in theory and practice; areas of rectilinear figures, and volumes of right parallelopipeds and prisms; the circle, sphere, cylinder, and cone; Mental Arithmetic.

9. *Algebra.*—Elementary rules; factoring; greatest common measure; least common multiple; fractions; simple equations of one, two, and three unknown quantities; simple problems.

10. *Euclid.*—Book I., with easy problems.

12. *Physics.*—The elements of Physics, as treated in Huxley's Introductory Science Primer and Balfour Stewart's Science Primer.

14. *Botany.*—The elements of structural Botany, including systematic examinations of common plants selected to show variety of structure in the different organs; true nature of the parts of the flower; various forms of roots, structure and uses, how distinguished from underground stems; various forms of stems, bulbs and tubers, herbs, shrubs and trees; nature and position of buds; forms and disposition of foliage leaves; kinds of inflorescence, special forms of flower-leaves, morphology of the calyx, corolla, stamens, and pistil; modifications of the flower due to adhesion, cohesion, and suppression of parts; classification of fruits; the seed and its parts; germination; the vegetable cell; protoplasm; chlorophyll; formation of new cells; various kinds of tissues; intercellular spaces; structure of leaves; exogenous and endogenous growth; food of plants; reproduction in flowering plants; nature of the pollen-grain; fertilization of the ovule; reproduction in ferns; the spore. Outlines of classification; examination and classification of common plants belonging to the following natural orders:—Ranunculaceæ, Cruciferæ, Malvaceæ, Leguminosæ, Rosaceæ, Sapindaceæ, Umbelliferæ, Compositæ, Labiatæ, Coniferæ, Araceæ Liliaceæ, Triliaceæ, Iridaceæ, Gramineæ; the characters and general properties of these orders.

15. *Latin.*—The Elementary Latin Book, grammar, composition, and the texts prescribed from time to time by the Education Department.

16. *Greek.*—The Elementary Greek Book.

17. *French.*—The Elementary French Book, grammar, composition, and the texts prescribed from time to time by the Education Department.

18. *German.*—The Elementary German Book, grammar, composition, and the texts prescribed from time to time by the Education Department.

19. *Writing.*

20. *Book-keeping.*—Single and double entry; commercial forms; general business transactions.

21. *Drawing.*—Freehand ; practical Geometry ; perspective ; industrial designs.

22. *Music.*—Vocal and Theoretical.

Form II.

1. *Reading.*—Course for Form I. continued.

2. *Orthography and Orthoëpy.*—Course for Form I. continued.

3. *English Grammar.*—Course for Form I. continued. (As prescribed for the Pass Matriculation Examination of the University of Toronto.)

4. *Composition.*—Course for Form I. continued.

5. *Literature.*—The critical study of the texts prescribed from time to time for the Pass Matriculation Examination of the University of Toronto.

6. *English History* (including Colonial History).—From William III. to George III., inclusive. Roman history from the commencement of the second Punic War to the death of Augustus. Greek history from the Persian to the Peloponnesian Wars, both inclusive (University Pass).

7. *Geography, Modern.*—North America and Europe. *Ancient.*—Greece, Italy, and Asia Minor (University Pass).

8. *Arithmetic.*—Course for Form I. continued (University Pass).

9. *Algebra.*—To the end of Quadratics (University Pass).

10. *Geometry.*—Euclid books I., II., III. ; easy deductions (University Pass).

12. *Physics.*—Definitions of velocity, acceleration, mass, momentum, force, moment, couple, energy, work, centre of inertia, statement of Newton's Laws of Motion, composition and resolution of forces, condition for equilibrium of forces in one plane. Definition of a fluid, fluid pressure at a point, transmission of fluid pressure, resultant fluid pressure, specific gravity, Boyle's Law, the barometer. air-pump, water-pump, siphon (University Matriculation Examination).

13. *Chemistry.*—Reynolds' Experimental Chemistry (chaps. I to XVI, inclusive).*

14. *Botany.*—Course in Form I. continued.

15. *Latin.*—Examination subjects as prescribed from time to time for Pass Matriculation into the University of Toronto.

16. *Greek*   "   "   "   "   "   "   "   "   "   "

17. *French*   "   "   "   "   "   "   "   "   "   "

18. *German*   "   "   "   "   "   "   "   "   "   "

---

* The text-book in Chemistry is intended to show teachers how the course is limited. It is not a text-book for pupils.

19. *Writing.*—Course for Form I. continued.

20. *Book-keeping and Commercial Transactions.*—Course for Form I. continued.

21. *Drawing.*—Course for Form I. continued.

22. *Music.*—   "   "   "

23. *Precis-writing and Indexing.*

24. *Phonography* (optional).

Form III.

3. *English Grammar.*—Course for Form II. continued.

4. *Composition.*   "   "   "   "   "   "

5. *Literature.*—The critical study of the texts prescribed from time to time for Honor Matriculation into the University, Toronto.

6. *History.*—English history under the Houses of Tudor and Stuart.

7. *Geography.*—The British Empire, including the colonies (Honor Matriculation University).

9. *Algebra.*—To the end of Binomial Theorem (Honor Matriculation University).

10.—*Geometry.*—Euclid, Books I, to IV. inclusive, Book VI. and definition of Book V. (Honor Matriculation University)

11. *Trigonometry.*—(Honor Matriculation University) The solution of Triangles.

13. *Chemistry.*—Reynolds' Experimental Chemistry, chaps. I. to XXVI. inclusive. (University Matriculation Examination.)

14. *Botany.*—The structure and classification of Canadian flowering plants. (University Matriculation Examination).

15. *Latin.*—Examination subjects as prescribed from time to time for Honor Matriculation into the University of Toronto.

16. *Greek*   "   "   "   "   "   "   "   "   "   "

17. *French*   "   "   "   "   "   "   "   "   "

18. *German*   "   "   "   "   "   "   "   "   "   "

Form IV.

99. The subjects for study in Form IV. shall be those now prescribed by the University of Toronto for Senior Matriculation, Pass and Honors. As far as possible, the classes shall be the same as those in Forms II. and III.

Commercial Course.

100. Candidates for a diploma in the Commercial Course will be examined at the same time and place, and on the same papers as candidates for second class non-professional certificates.

Graduation Diploma.

101. Any Pupil who passes the Departmental or the University examination in any of the courses herein prescribed for Forms II., III. or IV., in High Schools, shall be entitled to a Graduation Diploma signed by the Minister of Education and the Head Master of the High School at which such course was completed.

Certificates of Attendance and Character.

102. In addition to passing the prescribed examination, each candidate for a Graduation Diploma shall submit to the Education Department, through the Head Master, the following documents :—(1) A certificate from the Head Master that the candidate is a High School pupil who has attended for at least one year. (2) A certificate of character signed by the Head Master.

Presentation of Diplomas.

103. Commencement Exercises should be held in each High School or Collegiate Institute, at a suitable time during the Autumn term of each year, at which the Graduation Diplomas may be presented to the successful candidates.

Duties of Teachers and Pupils.

104. The regulations respecting the duties of teachers and pupils in High Schools shall be the same as those affecting teachers and pupils in Public Schools, except as herein otherwise provided.

Qualifications of Head Masters and Assistants.

105. The qualifications for the Headmastership of a High School or Collegiate Institute shall be (*a*) a degree in Arts obtained after a regular course of study from any chartered university in the British Dominions, and (*b*) one year's successful teaching either as assistant master in a High School or in a College or a Private School.

106. After the first day of July, 1885, no one shall be deemed qualified for the position of High School Assistant unless he hold a First Class Professional Public School Certificate ; or unless he be a Graduate in Arts (as above), or an Undergraduate in Arts of at least two years' standing, who has obtained a professional certificate at a Training Institute.

107. Any teacher who is not qualified as above, but who, on the first day of July, 1885, is employed as an Assistant in a High School or Collegiate Institute, shall be deemed a legally qualified Assistant for such High School, but for no other.

INSPECTION.

108. It shall be the duty of each High School Inspector to visit the High Schools or Collegiate Institutes in the section of the Province assigned to him, at least once in each year; to spend not less than one day in each school having two or three masters; and in schools with four or over four masters, to spend two or more days, as the interests of the school may require.

109. At each visit he shall ascertain by means of an oral or a written examination the standing of the pupils in the departments of English, Classics, Mathematics, Modern Languages and Science; and shall also make enquiry and examination, in such manner as he may think proper, into the efficiency of the staff, the equipment of the school, and all matters affecting the health and comfort of the pupils.

110. He shall report to the Department, one week after his inspection, the result of his observations and enquiry on a form prescribed for that purpose, and in the case of a Collegiate Institute he shall make a special report based on the regulations under which Collegiate Institutes are established, setting forth in detail any departure from the said regulations.

111. No High School Inspector shall, during his incumbency, hold any office or perform any other duties than those assigned to or prescribed for him, without the permission of the Department.

DISTRIBUTION OF GRANT.

112. On and after the first of July, 1886, the Annual Legislative Grants to High Schools and Collegiate Institutes shall be distributed on the following basis, so far as the annual appropriation made by the Legislature will admit thereof, namely :—

I.—*Two Masters' Schools.*

(a) Fixed grant $400 00

(b) Grant on annual expenditure for teachers' salaries:—20% on salaries over $1,500 00, *max*.................................... 100 00

(c) Grant on total amount invested in equipment :—10% of expenditure [detailed by the High School Boards to the Education Department (in a form to be provided) and *annually* certified and approved by the High School Inspectors] on the following bases, the maximum recognized expenditure on each being also as follows :—

(1) Library of reference $275 00
(2) Scientific apparatus, physical
     and chemical (not including
     chemicals) 275 00
(3) Gymnasium and equipment ..   250 00
(4) Charts, maps, and globes 100 00
                              max.   90 00

(*d*) Grant on condition and suitability of school
     premises :—

    (1) Water-closets, water supply, school grounds,
       and external appearance of school-
       building.*

    (2) Class-rooms, halls, waiting-rooms, cap-
       rooms, teachers' private rooms, desks,
       blackboards, lighting, heating, and
       ventilation.
                              max.   90 00

(*e*) Grant on average attendance, being 50c. per
     unit.

II.—*Three or more Masters' Schools (not Institutes).*

(*a*) Fixed grant.......................... $400 00

(*b*) Grant on annual expenditure for teachers'
     salaries:—

    (1) Twenty % on salaries over $1,500 00 *max.*   100 00
    (2) Twenty-five %   "   " $2,000 00   "   500 00

(*c*) Grant on total amount invested in equip-
     ment:—10% of expenditure [detailed by
     the High Boards to the Education Depart-
     ment (in a form to be provided) and
     annually certified and approved by the
     High School Inspectors] on the following
     bases, the maximum recognized expendi-
     ture in each being also as follows :—

    (1) Library of reference $450 00
    (2) Scientific apparatus, physical
       and chemical (not including
       chemicals)..............   450 00
    (3) Gymnasium and equipment ..   325 00
    (4) Charts, maps, and globes 125 00
                              max.   135 00

(*d*) Grant on condition and suitability of school
     premises :—

(1) Water-closets, water supply, school grounds, and external appearance of school-building.*

(2) Class-rooms, halls, waiting-rooms, cap-rooms, teachers' private rooms, desks, blackboards, lighting, heating, and ventilation.*

max. 135 00

(e) Grant on average attendance, being 50c. per unit.

III.—Collegiate Institutes.

(a) Fixed grant............................ $400 00

(b) Grant on expenditure for teachers' salaries:—

(1) Twenty % on salaries over $1,500 00 *max.* 100 00
(2) Twenty-five % "   "   2,000 00 " 500 00
(3) Twenty % "   "   4,000 00 " 500 00

(c) Grant on condition and suitability of school-premises :—

(1) Water-closets, water supply, school grounds, and external appearance of school-building.*

(2) Class-rooms, halls, waiting-rooms, cap-rooms, teachers' private-rooms, desks, blackboards, lighting, heating, and ventilation.*

max. 180 00

(d) Grant on average attendance, being 50c. per unit.

(e) Special grant, based partly on equipment and partly on qualifications of staff 250 00

COUNTY MODEL SCHOOLS.

General Conditions.

113. The County Board of Examiners for each county or group of counties shall set apart at least one Public School as a Model School for

---

* A maximum will be determined, and classes recognized, under each sub-head.

3

the professional training of Third Class Teachers, subject to the approval of the Education Department.

114. In order to entitle a Public School to be ranked and used for Model School purposes, the following conditions must be complied with:—

(1) The Principal must hold a First Class Provincial Certificate and have at least three years' experience as a Public School teacher.

(2) There must be at least three assistants holding Second Class Provincial Certificates.

(3) The equipment of the school must be equal to that required by the regulations for the fourth class of a Public School.

(4) A room for Model School purposes, in addition to the accommodation required for the Public School, must be provided, either in the same building or elsewhere.

(5) An assistant must be employed to relieve the Principal of Public School work during at least half the day while the Model School is in session.

115. The teachers in training shall attend regularly and punctually during the whole Model School term, and shall be subject to the discipline of the Principal, with an appeal, in case of dispute, to the Chairman of the County Board of Examiners.

116. The Principal shall report at the close of the session the status of each teacher in training, as shown by the daily register.

117. The teachers in training shall be subjected to an examination in practical teaching at the close of the session, and also to a written examination on papers prepared by the Department.

118. In any county where there are two or more Model Schools the County Board shall distribute the students equally among the different schools, and in cases where there may be a deficiency of room in any Model School to accommodate all the students, the County Board may give the preference of admission to such as have gained the highest number of marks at the non-professional examination.

119. Boards of Trustees may impose a fee of not more than five dollars on each teacher in training, and in addition thereto the County Board of Examiners may impose a fee not exceeding two dollars per student as an examination fee in lieu of the amount chargeable against the county for conducting the professional examination.

120. There shall be one session of thirteen weeks in each Model School during the year, beginning on the second Tuesday in September.

121. Each Model School shall be visited at least once during the session by the Departmental Inspector.

Course of Study.

122. The course of study in County Model Schools shall embrace the following:—

(1) *Principles of Education.*—School organization, management, discipline, methods of instruction, and practice in teaching.

(2) *Practical Teaching.*—Such practice in teaching as will cultivate correct methods of presenting subjects to a class and develop the art of school government.

(3) *Physiology and Hygiene.*—(a)—Laws of health, temperance, cleanliness, hours for study, rest, recreation, and sleep. (b)—Heating and ventilation of the school-room. (c)—Functions of the brain, eye, stomach, heart and lungs.

(4) *Music, Drawing and Calisthenics.*—As prescribed for the Fourth Class of Public Schools.

(5) *Review of Non-Professional Work.*—A review of the principal subjects in the Public School curriculum, such as composition, grammar, arithmetic and literature.

(6) *School Law.*—A knowledge of school law, so far as it relates to the duties of teachers and pupils.

Text Books.

123. Every teacher in training shall supply himself with the following text books:—1. A complete set of all the text books prescribed for use in the first four classes of a Public School. 2. Baldwin's Art of School Management. 3. Oscar Browning's Educational Theories.

Final Examination.

124. At the close of the term an examination shall be held by the County Board of Examiners, who shall also determine the minimum marks of each candidate, subject to an appeal to the Education Department. The results of this examination, together with the report of the the Principal, will determine the final standing of each student. Although music and drill are optional the Board of Examiners should see that due credit is given for attainments in these subjects. The final examination shall be conducted on the following subjects:

	Marks.
Education (theory)	100
Education (methods)	100
Practical teaching	100
Physiology and Hygiene......................	100
School Law and Regulations.................	50
Drawing......................................	50
Music (optional)	50
Drill and Calisthenics (optional)	50

TEACHERS' INSTITUTES.

125. In each county or inspectoral division, a Teachers' Institute shall be formed, the object of which shall be to read papers and discuss matters having a practical bearing on the daily work of the schoolroom.

126. The officers of the Institute shall be a president, vice-president, and secretary-treasurer. There shall also be a management committee of five. The officers of the Institute and the management committee shall be elected annually.

127. There shall be at least one meeting of the Institute each year, extending over two or more days, to be called the annual meeting, for the election of officers and the discussion of such matters as may be submitted by the management committee.

128. The session of the annual meeting on the first day shall be from 10 a.m. to 12 m., and from 2 p.m. to 5 p.m. ; on the second day from 9 a.m. to 12 m., and from 2 p.m. to 4 p.m.

129. The time and place for holding the annual meeting and the programme for the same, will be arranged by the Education Department on consultation with the Inspector or Inspectors of the county or divisional Institute. A copy of the programme should be sent to every teacher in the county or inspectoral division, at least one month before the time of the meeting. All questions and discussions foreign to the Teachers' work should be avoided.

130. A portion of the afternoon of the second day should be set apart for discussing such matters as affect the relations between the Teacher and the Trustees, of which special notice should be given to every Board of Trustees in the county or inspectoral division.

131. Another meeting, arrangements for which should be made at the annual meeting of the Institute, for the county or inspectoral division, may be held during the year; or in lieu thereof a series of Township Institutes may be held in the townships or union of townships in the county.

132. It shall be the duty of every teacher to attend continuously all the meetings of the Institute held in his county or inspectoral division (two days in each half year so spent to be counted as visiting days). and in the event of his inability so to attend, he shall report to his Inspector, giving reasons for his absence.

133. It shall be the duty of the Inspector to furnish the secretary of the Institute with a list of the teachers in his county or inspectoral division. From this list the roll shall be called at the opening of each session. He shall also report to the Department on the form prescribed.

134. The following order of business is recommended.

First Day.

1. Opening.
2. Appointment of committees.
3. Business.
4. Reading and discussion of papers.
5. Lecture in the evening by the Departmental Director of Teachers' Institutes.

Second Day.

1. Opening.
2. Receiving report of Committees.
3. Business.
4. Reading and discussion of papers.
5. Election of Officers.
6. Closing.

135. The Departmental Director of Teachers' Institutes shall attend the annual meeting of each Institute, and shall discuss at least three subjects on the programme, and deliver a public lecture on the evening of the first day.

————

PROVINCIAL NORMAL AND MODEL SCHOOLS.

General.

136. There shall be two sessions of the Provincial Normal Schools in ecah year:—The first, opening on the third Tuesday in January, and closing on the third Friday in June; the second, opening on the third Tuesday in August, and closing not later than the twenty-second of December.

137. The hours of daily work shall be from 9 a.m. to 12, and from 1.30 p.m. to 4 p.m. The daily sessions shall be opened and closed as prescribel in the Regulations for Public Schools

138. The students shall lodge and board at such houses only as are approved by the Principal; and shall not be out of their boarding-house after 9.30 p.m. Ladies and gentlemen shall not board at the same house. Communication of every kind between the sexes is strictly prohibited.

Duties of the Principal.

139. The Principal shall be responsible for the discipline, classification and organization of the Normal School students; he shall prescribe the duties of the Masters, subject to the approval of the Minister of Education ; he shall cause such examinations to be held from time to time as may be deemed necessary, and keep a record of the same ; he shall give such directions to the officers of the Normal School as will secure the efficiency of the service.

Duties of the Masters.

140. The Masters shall be responsible to the Principal for the order, discipline, and general progress of their classes ; they shall report monthly to the Principal the standing of each student in the subjects of their departments, and, daily, the absence of any student from their classes.

Duties of Students.

141. Every student shall attend regularly and punctually all the classes during the term ; he shall conduct himself with becoming courtesy towards his teachers and fellow-students ; he shall make reparation for all damage caused by him to furniture or other property belonging to the school, and he shall submit to such discipline as may be required by the Principal or Masters of the Normal School.

Course of Study.

142. The course of study in the Normal Schools shall embrace the history, science and art of education, school organization and management, school hygiene, practical English and English literature, natural science, mathematics, drawing and writing, music, drill and calisthenics, as defined in the Syllabus of Lectures prescribed by the Education Department.

Practical Teaching.

143. Every student shall be required to conduct classes in the Model School, and to teach such subjects as he may be directed, under the supervision of the teachers of the Normal and Model School.

Examinations.

144. At the close of each term an Examination shall be held by Examiners appointed by the Minister of Education. The results of this Examination and of the Examinations held during the term, together with the Reports of the Principal and Masters of the Normal School, and the Teachers of the Model School, shall determine the final standing of each student. A minimum of forty per cent. of the marks obtainable in each subject and 60 per cent. of the aggregate marks shall be required to entitle the student to a certificate.

Subjects for Final Examination.

SUBJECT.	TIME.	MARKS ALLOWED.
History of Education	1 hour.	100
Science of Education	"	150
Principles and Practice of Education	"	150
School Organization and School Management	"	150
English Literature	"	100
Practical English	"	100
Hygiene	"	100
Chemistry	"	100
Physics	"	100
Botany	"	100
Zoology	"	100
Drawing	"	100
Writing	"	100
Music	"	100
Calisthenics	"	100
Drill	"	100
Language Lessons, Grammar, etc.	"	150
Reading	"	100
Arithmetic	"	150
Algebra	"	100
Practical Teaching in Model School	"	500

Model School.

145. The Masters of the Model School, shall act under the direction of the Principal of the Normal School, and shall be responsible to him for the order, discipline and progress of the pupils attending the Model School.

146. The terms of the Model Schools shall correspond to those in High Schools, and except, to fill up vacancies, pupils shall be admitted only at the beginning of a term.

147. The Regulations respecting pupils in Public and High Schools shall apply to the pupils of the Model School, subject to such variations as may be approved by the Minister of Education on the report of the Principal.

COUNTY BOARD OF EXAMINERS.

148. In every county there shall be a Board of Examiners for examining candidates for Third Class Professional Certificates, and for such other purposes as are prescribed in the Public School Act, consisting of the Inspector or Inspectors of the County, and the Inspector of any city or town within the territorial limits of the county, and two other persons appointed by the County Council.

149. Any person having three years' experience as a teacher in a Public or High School, and who holds (a) a First Class Provincial Certificate, or (b) a Degree in Arts from any chartered University in the Province of Ontario, or (c) a Certificate as Head Master of a High School, shall be eligible to be appointed a member of a County Board of Examiners.

150. The Board shall be organized by the appointment of a Chairman and Secretary, and accurate minutes of the proceedings of every meeting shall be entered in a book provided for that purpose.

151. The Chairman shall call meetings of the Board for the transaction of such business as may lawfully be brought before it; he shall preside at all meetings of the Board, but in his absence the other members of the Board may elect a Chairman.

152. The County Board of Examiners shall—

(a) Investigate all appeals against the action of any Inspector within their jurisdiction who suspends a teacher's certificate, and, where such suspension refers to a Third Class certificate, they shall confirm or set aside such appeal, but in the case of a First or Second Class certificate, they shall report to the Minister of Education ;

(b) Conduct the professional examination of the Third Class teachers at the close of the Model School term, and award certificates valid for three years, and report the result to the Education Department ;

(c) Exercise a general supervision over the County Model School and make recommendations in regard to its location, continuance or improvement, as they may deem expedient.

153. Where the County Council appoints two members to conduct examinations in French or German, as provided in section 170 of the Public School Act, such additional persons shall be members of the Board for all purposes prescribed in the said School Act and in the regulations herein set forth.

154. In preparing examination papers for candidates who write in the French or German language, the standard prescribed for entrance to High Schools shall, as near as possible, be adopted by the examiners.

155. In addition to the examination conducted in the French or German language every candidate for a teacher's certificate shall be required to pass such examinations in English Grammar and in translation from French or German into English as may be required by the Board of Examiners.

156. A fee not exceeding two dollars may be imposed by the County Board of Examiners on each candidate at the professional examination, in lieu of the allowances prescribed in section 171 of the Public School Act.

TEACHERS' CERTIFICATES.

157. Certificates to teach a Public School shall rank as of the First, Second or Third Class; those of the First Class shall be sub-divided into grades A, B, and C; those of the Second and Third Class shall be each of one grade only. Third Class Certificates shall be valid for three years.

158. There shall be two examinations for granting certificates, one for testing the literary attainments of the candidates, to be known as the non-professional examination; the other at a County Model School for Third Class teachers;—at a Provincial Normal School for Second Class teachers;—and at a Training Institute for First Class Teachers, to be known as the Professional Examination for each class respectively.

159. The holder of the Ontario Art School Certificate, grade B, will be exempted from the examination herein prescribed in Drawing for Non-Professional Certificates of every class and grade.

Third Class Non-Professional Certificates.

160. Candidates for a Third Class Non-Professional Teachers' Certificate will be examined in the following subjects as prescribed for Form I. of the High School Course of Study, viz:—Nos. 1-10, 19, 20 and 21, with an option between 15, 17, 18, and group 12 and 14.

161. When a Third Class certificate has expired, the holder thereof may, on passing the Departmental examination, obtain a renewal of the same for a period of three years, subject to attendance at a County Model School, at the discretion of the County Board of Examiners.

162. In the case of such applicants for a renewal of Third Class Certificates as take the minimum number of marks in each subject, but fail in the aggregate, a bonus not exceeding 200 marks for efficiency and aptitude in teaching may be allowed on the report and at the discretion of the County Inspector.

163. A holder of a Third Class Certificate who passes the Non-Professional examination for any certificate of a higher grade shall, on application to the County Board of Examiners, and on proof of his efficiency as a teacher, be entitled to have such Third Class Certificate extended, by endorsement, for a period not exceeding three years from the date of such examination but no certificate shall be extended for a longer period than three years without re-examination.

164 In case of an emergency, such as a scarcity of teachers, or for any other special cause, Third Class Certificates may be extended by the Minister of Education, on the joint request of any Board of Trustees and the County Inspector; but all such extensions shall be limited to the school on whose behalf the request is made.

165. A temporary certificate may be given by the County Inspector under the conditions stated in regulation 51 (14).

Second Class Non-Professional Certificates.

166. Candidates for a Second Class Non-Professional Teachers' Certificate will be examined in the following subjects as prescribed for Form II. of the High School Course of Study, excepting Ancient History and Geography, viz.:—Nos. 1-10, 13, 21, with an option between 15, 17, 18, group 12 and 14, and group 19, 20, and 23. Candidates who do not take the commercial option for Second Class, shall pass the Third Class Non-Professional examination in Nos. 19 and 20.

First Class Non-Professional Certificates—Grade C.

167. Candidates for a First Class Non-Professional Certificate Grade C will be examined in the following subjects as prescribed for Form III. of the High School Course, viz.:—Nos. 3, 4, 5, 6, 7, 9, 10, 11, 13 and 14 of Form III., and also 12 of Form II. At the examination in Botany, candidates will be expected to describe and classify a submitted specimen of a Canadian flowering plant. Only such candidates as pass the Second Class Non-Professional examination will be eligible to write for First "C," but both examinations may be taken the same year.

168. Candidates who, in addition to the Departmental Second Class Non-professional examination, have passed the junior matriculation examination of Toronto University with first class honors in Mathematics, English, and History and Geography, or an equivalent examination in any of the chartered Universities of Ontario, shall be awarded a First C Non-professional certificate without further examination.

Grades A and B.—Non-Professional.

169. Candidates for a Departmental Certificate, Grade A or B, taking the Departmental examinations, shall not be eligible to write for this grade until they have first passed the examination required for Grade C, but nothing herein contained shall prevent a candidate from writing at both examinations the same year. A candidate for Grade A or B will be allowed an option between English and Mathematics.

170. Graduates in Arts who have proceeded regularly to their degree, and who, at their final examination, have taken First or Second Class Honors in one of the departments of Science, Classics, Mathematics or Modern Languages, or in the department of Mental and Moral Science and Civil

Polity, shall, on application to the Education Department, receive a First Class Non-Professional Certificate, grade A or B according as the Honors were First or Second Class.

171. Non-Professional examinations for First Class Certificates, Grade A or B, shall be limited as follows:—

Department of English.

Composition.—History and Etymology of the English Language; Rhetorical Forms; Prosody.

Books of Reference; Earle's Philology of the English Tongue; Abbot and Seeley's English for English People; Bain's Composition and Rhetoric, or Hill's Rhetoric; Marsh's English Language and Literature, Lectures VI. to XI. inclusive.

Literature :

1. History of English Literature, from Chaucer to the end of the reign of James I. Books of Reference: Craik's History of the English Literature and Language, or Arnold's Literature, English Edition; Marsh's English Language and Literature, Lectures VI. to XI. inclusive.

2. Specified works of standard authors as prescribed from time to time by the Department.

History :

Greece.—The Persian to the Peloponnesian War inclusive.—Cox's History of Greece (unabridged).

Rome.—From the beginning of the Second Punic War to the death of Julius Cæsar.—Mommsen's History of Rome.

England.—The Tudor and Stuart Periods, as presented in Green's Short History of the English People, Macaulay's History of England (or Franck Bright's History of England, Second Volume), and Hallam's Constitutional History.

Canada—Parkman's Old Regime in Canada and Wolfe and Montcalm.

Geography :

So much Ancient Geography as is necessary for the proper understanding of the portions of the Histories of Greece and Rome prescribed.

Department of Mathematics.

Algebra.—Symmetry, Binomial Theorem, Multinomial Theorem, Exponential and Logarithmic Series, Interest and Annuities, Indeterminate Coefficients; Partial Fractions, Series (Convergency and Divergency,

Reversion, Summation), Inequalities, Determinants as far as in Gross, Reduction and Resolution of Equations of first four Degrees and of Binomial Equations, Relations between Roots and Coefficients of Equations, Indeterminate Equations, Problems.

Analytical Plane Geometry.—The Point (including Transformation of Co-ordinates), the Right Line, the Circle, the Parabola, the Ellipse, the Hyperbola, the General Equation of the Second Degree, Abridged Notation.

Trigonometry.— Trigonometrical Equations, Solution of Triangles, Measurement of Heights and Distances; Inscribed, Circumscribed, and Escribed Circles of a Triangle; Quadrilaterals, Description of Vernier and Theodolite, Trigonometrical and Logarithmic Tables, Demoivre's Theorem.

Statics.—Equilibrium of Forces acting in one plane ; Parallelogram of Forces, Parallel Forces, Moments, Couples, Centre of Gravity, Virtual Work, Machines, Friction, Experimental Verifications.

Dynamics.—Measurement of Velocities and of Acceleration, Laws of Motion, Energy, Momentum, Uniform and Uniformly Accelerated Motion, Falling Bodies, Moments of Inertia, Uniform Circular Motion, Projectiles in Vacuo, Collisions, Simple Pendulum, Experimental Verifications.

Elementary Geometrical Optics.—Reflection and Refraction of Light at Plane and Spherical Surfaces, including Prisms and Lenses (aberration not considered); the Eye ; Construction and use of the more simple Instruments

The following books are recommended for reference in addition to those prescribed for grade C:—

Algebra.—Gross & Todhunter.

Analytical Geometry.—Vyvyan and C. Smith.   Refer to Salmon.

Trigonometry.—Hamblin Smith ; Refer to Colenso or Todhunter.

Dynamics.—Garnet, or Gross's Kinematics and Kinetics.

Geometrical Optics.—Aldis.

Valuation of Subjects for First, C, Second and Third Class Non-Professional Certificates.

172. The values of the different subjects in which candidates for Non-Professional Certificates will be examined, shall be as follows :—Reading (oral), 50 marks ; Reading, Principles of, 50 ; Orthography and Orthoëpy, 50 : English Grammar, 150 ; Composition, 100 ; Literature, Poetry and

Prose, 200; History, 100; Geography, 75; Arithmetic, written and Mental, 200; Algebra, 100; Geometry, 100; Trigonometry, 100; Physics, Chemistry and Botany, each, 100; Latin, French, and German, each, 200; Writing, Book-Keeping and Commercial transactions, Precis-writing and Indexing, 200; Drawing, 75.

173. Any candidate who obtains one-third of the marks in each subject, and one-half of the aggregate marks obtainable, shall be entitled to rank as the holder of a non-professional certificate of the class for which he is such candidate.

Professional Certificates.

174. The holder of a Third Class Non-Professional Certificate, who takes the course and passes the examination prescribed for County Model Schools, shall be entitled to rank as a Third Class Teacher of Public Schools.

175. The holder of a Second Class Non-Professional Certificate, who has taught a Public School successfully for one year, and who attends a Provincial Normal School one session, and passes the prescribed examina-tion, shall be entitled to rank as a Second Class Teacher of Public Schools.

176. Any Graduate in Arts with Honors as prescribed in Regulation, 170, or the holder of a First Class Non-Professional Certificate, who has passed an examination at a Provincial Normal School, and who attends a Training Institute one Session and passes the prescribed examination thereat, shall be entitled to rank as a First Class Teacher of Public Schools or an Assistant Master of High Schools.

177. Any teacher who holds a First Class Non-Professional Certificate and a Second Class Professional Certificate, and who has taught success-fully for at least two years in a Public School, High School, or Collegiate Institute, shall be entitled to rank as a First Class Teacher or Assistant Master of a High School, on passing the final examination prescribed for a Training Institute, without attendance thereat.

DISTRICT CERTIFICATES.

178. The Boards of Examiners, constituted under section 163 of the Public Schools' Act of 1885, may issue Certificates, valid only in such portions of their respective district or districts as they may deem expedient, for a period not exceeding three years.

179. The Board of Examiners shall prepare the examination papers, fix the time and place for holding the examinations, read and value the answers, determine the fees to be paid by candidates, and generally exercise all the powers of County Board of Examiners.

180. Each Board of Examiners shall, as soon after the examination as possible, report to the Minister the names and residences of the Candidates examined, the number of Certificates granted, and enclose therewith a full set of the examination papers.

181. The District Board is authorized to require attendance at a County Model School, or such other professional training as may be deemed expedient.

182. The members of District Boards of Examiners shall be entitled to the same remuneration as the members of County Boards. Where county organization exists, all the expenses of the examinations, so far as they may not be covered by fees, shall be paid by the County Council.

ANNUAL DEPARTMENTAL EXAMINATIONS.

General.

183. The examination papers for the Departmental Examinations shall be prepared by the Central Committee of Examiners.

184. Each paper shall be approved by the whole Committee at a regular meeting called for that purpose, and shall bear the name of an examiner.

185. The papers on each subject shall be limited strictly to the Course of Study prescribed in the regulations, and shall be placed in the Minister's hands not later than the first day of March in each year.

186. The Minister of Education shall appoint such sub-examiners as may be deemed necessary to read and value the answers of candidates— such sub-examiners to work under the direction of, and to report to, the Central Committee.

187. Except when special qualifications are required, no person will be considered eligible for the position of sub-examiner unless he possess the qualifications at least of a member of a County Board of Examiners. No person shall serve as sub-examiner for more than three years continuously.

188. Each sub-examiner shall be paid the sum of six dollars per day under the restriction that the whole amount paid for the examination shall not exceed the sum of one dollar for each candidate.

189. The hours for work shall be from 8.30 a.m. to 12, noon, and from 2 p.m. to 5.30 p.m., and no sub-examiner shall make up lost time or read examination papers at any other hours.

Time and Place of Examination.

190. The examination of candidates for Departmental Certificates shall be held in the month of July, in each year, on the days appointed by the Minister of Education.

191. Candidates for First Class Certificates of all grades, will be examined at the Normal School, Toronto; candidates for Second and Third Class Certificates will be examined at their respective High Schools, or at such other places as may be appointed by the Minister of Education.

192. Where a High School is situated in a town or city constituting a separate Inspectoral division, the Inspector of such city or town shall be responsible for the conduct of the examination held thereat, and shall receive applications from intending candidates, and report to the Department, but in all other cases the County Inspector shall be responsible and receive the necessary applications.

Notice to be given by Candidates, etc.

193 Every person who purposes to present himself at any examination for a Second or a Third Class Certificate shall send to the Inspector, within whose inspectoral division he intends to write not later than the 1st of June preceding, a notice stating the class of certificate for which he is a candidate, and what optional subject or subjects he has selected.

194. Such notice shall be accompanied by a fee of $2 for each certificate for which the candidate proposes to write, one half of which shall be forwarded, by the Inspector, with the list of candidates, to the Education Department, and the other half to the Treasurer of the High School Board.

195. Every person intending to write for a First Class Certificate shall notify the Education Department, such notice to be accompanied by a fee of $2.

196. The Inspector shall preside at and be responsible for the proper conduct of the examination, but in case of his inability to attend he shall send to the Education Department for the approval of the Minister, one month before the examination, the name of the person whom he intends to appoint as his substitute, otherwise the Department will make the appointment. When more rooms than one are required for the candidates, a presiding Examiner, approved by the Minister, must be appointed for each room, and the Examiner, in his report to the Department, shall indicate the candidates who were placed in the several rooms respectively.

197. The Inspector shall not nominate as his substitute any teacher employed in a school from which there is any candidate at such examination, or any person who has taken part in the instruction of any of the candidates; nor shall any such person be appointed as presiding Examiner, or be present with the candidates, in any room at such examination; and at least one Examiner shall be present during the whole time of the examination, in each room occupied by the candidates.

198. Every Inspector shall send to the Education Department, not later than the 2nd of June, a list of the names, with the fees, of those who intend to present themselves for examination. To each name the Department will affix a number, which must be employed by the candidate instead of his usual signature, throughout the entire examination.

199. Each Inspector, or such other person as may be appointed by the Minister, shall himself in person receive from the Department, or Inspector, the examination papers, and shall thereupon be responsible for the safe-keeping of the parcel containing the same, unopened, until the morning of the first day of the examination.

200. No presiding Examiner shall admit any candidate, either as an additional candidate, or in the place of any absent one, whose notice has not been duly given to the Department; no candidate who, in his notice to the Department, elects to take any specific optional subject, will be allowed to substitute any other; no candidate who has given notice to the Department of his intention to be examined at a specified place, will be allowed to appear for examination elsewhere.

201. Each candidate shall satisfy the presiding Examiner as to his personal identity before the commencement of the second day's examination and any person detected in attempting to personate a candidate should be reported to the Department.

202. The Inspector or presiding Examiner shall transmit to the Education Department on the first day of the examination, a copy of the following declaration, signed by himself and the other Examiners (but such declaration shall not be required more than once from any Examiner):

"I solemnly declare that I will perform my duty of Examiner without fear, favour, affection or partiality towards any candidate."

Mode of Conducting Examinations.

203. Places should be allotted to the candidates for certificates so that they may be at least five feet apart. All diagrams or maps having reference to the subjects of examination shall be removed from the room; all arrangements shall be completed, and the necessary stationery distributed at least *fifteen* minutes before the time appointed for the commencement of the examination.

204. Candidates shall be in their allotted places before the hour appointed for the commencement of the examination. If a candidate be not present till after the appointed time, he shall not be allowed any additional time. No candidate shall be permitted, on any pretence whatever, to enter the room after the expiration of an hour from the commencement of the examination.

205. No candidate shall be allowed to leave the room within *one hour* after the issue of the examination papers in any subject; and if he then leave he shall not be permitted to return during the examination on the subject in hand.

206. Punctually at the time appointed for the commencement of the examination, the presiding Examiner shall, in the examination room, and in the presence of the candidates, break the seal of the envelope containing the examination papers for the first subject, and give them to the candidates. The papers of only one subject shall be opened at one time.

207. Every candidate shall conduct himself in strict accordance with the regulations, and should he give or receive any aid, or extraneous assistance of any kind, in answering the examination questions, he will be liable not only to the loss of the whole examination, but to the forfeiture or withdrawal of his certificate at any time afterward when the discovery is made that such aid or assistance has been given or received.

208. Should any candidate be detected in copying from another or allowing another to copy from him, or in taking into the room any book, notes, or anything from which he might derive assistance in the examination, or in talking or whispering, it shall be the duty of the presiding Examiner, if he obtain clear evidence of the fact at the time of its occurrence, to cause such candidate at once to leave the room; neither shall such candidate be permitted to enter during the remaining part of the examination, and his name shall be struck off the list. If, however, the evidence be not clear at the time, or be obtained after the conclusion of the examination, the Examiner shall report the case to the Department.

209. Every candidate shall write his NUMBER (not his name) very distinctly at the top of each page of his answer papers, in the middle; and is warned that for every page not bearing his number he is liable to receive no credit from the Examiners. If a candidate write his name or initials, or any distinguishing sign or mark on his paper other than the number assigned him by the Department, his paper will be cancelled.

210. Candidates, in preparing their answers, shall write on one side only of each sheet, and shall mark the sheets in each subject, as 1st, 2nd, 3rd, etc.; and on the last sheet shall write distinctly the total number of sheets enclosed in the envelope, and thus prevent any question arising as to the number of sheets actually put into each envelope. Having written the distinguishing NUMBER on each page, and having arranged the answer papers in the order of the questions, they shall fold them once across, place them in the envelopes provided by the Department, and write on the outside of the envelopes their numbers and the subjects of Examination. They shall then securely fasten the envelopes and hand them to the presiding Examiner.

211. Punctually at the expiration of the time allowed, the Examiner shall direct the candidates to stop writing, and cause them to hand in their answer papers immediately, duly fastened in the envelopes.

212. The Presiding Examiner shall keep upon his desk the certified list of the candidates and as each paper in any subject is handed in he shall check the same by entering the figure "1" opposite the name of the candidate on the form provided.

213. After the papers are handed in, the Examiner shall not allow any alterations to be made in them, and he shall be responsible for their safe keeping until he has transmitted them, with all surplus examination papers, to the Education Department.

214. The presiding Examiner, at the close of the examination on the last day, shall secure in a separate parcel the fastened envelopes of the candidates, and on the same day shall forward by express (pre-paid), or deliver to the Education Department, the package containing all the parcels thus separately secured. The papers are to be arranged by subjects and in numerical order. The Inspector or presiding Examiner shall, at the same time, sign and forward a solemn declaration that the examinations have been held and conducted in strict conformity with the regulations, and fairly and properly in every respect; and also a certificate, that he has been satisfied as to the personal identity of each candidate.

215 The Inspector or presiding Examiner (as the case may be), shall appoint an Examiner in Reading who shall hear each candidate read, from an authorized Reader, one passage selected by the Examiner, and another from any book, chosen by the candidate. The result, on the form provided, shall be transmitted to the Department.

216. The Treasurer of the High School Board, on the Certificate of the County Inspector, shall pay all the expenses of the Examination, including the sum of three dollars per day and actual travelling expenses, for the Inspector and presiding Examiners.

217. If an examination is held at a Public School then such fees as are herein mentioned shall be paid to the Treasurer of the Public School Board, who shall also upon the order of the Inspector pay all the expenses of the Examination.

Appeals.

218. A candidate for a non-professional certificate of the *Second* or the *Third* Class, may claim to have his papers re-read, upon the following conditions:—

(1) Such appeal or claim must be in the hands of the Minister on or before the 15th day of September; and the ground of the appeal or claim must be specifically stated.

(2) A deposit of two dollars must be made with the Department, which deposit will be returned to the candidate if his appeal or claim is sustained, but otherwise it will be forfeited.

(3) The Central Committee of Examiners shall meet on the earliest possible day after the 15th of September, and shall dispose of all the appeals without delay; and no appeal shall subsequently be entertained on any ground whatever.

TRAINING INSTITUTES.

Requisites of a Training Institute.

219. The requisites of a Training Institute shall be as follows:—

(a) Such equipment and accommodation as may be required for a Collegiate Institute.

(b) A staff of thoroughly competent specialists in the Modern Languages, Mathematics, Classics, and Science; and, in addition, teachers competent to give instruction in Music, Drawing, and Drill and Calisthenics.

General.

220. Application for admission to a Training Institute shall be made, on or before the first Monday in September, to the Minister of Education, who will assign to each Training Institute its quota of teachers-in-training.

221. There shall be each year in every Training Institute one session of fourteen weeks, beginning on the second Monday of September, and ending on the second Friday of December.

222. The hours of daily attendance for each teacher-in-training shall in each case be determined by the Principal of the Training Institute, who shall make such arrangements as may best suit the requirements of his school, subject, however, to the regulations hereinafter provided.

223. Each Training Institute shall be inspected by one of the High School Inspectors at least once during the session. It shall be the Inspector's duty to report to the Minister of Education on the condition of the Training Institute, and to make such recommendations as he may consider necessary to secure its efficiency.

224. The term Department Master, as used in these regulations, shall be held to mean the Master of the department of English, Mathematics, Science, Modern Languages, or Classics, or of any sub-department thereof.

Course of Study and Training.

225. The course of study and training to be followed in each Training Institute shall be as follows:—

(*a*) The History of Education.

(*b*) The Science of Education.

(*c*) The Principles and Practice of Teaching with especial reference to High School work.

(*d*) The organization and management of schools with especial reference to the different grades of High Schools.

(*e*) Systematic observation of the mode of conducting a High School.

(*f*) Practice in managing classes and in teaching the High School course under the supervision of the Principal and his staff.

(*g*) Special instruction by the Principal and the Department Masters.

(*h*) Hygiene; School-law in reference to the duties of teachers and pupils.

Duties of the Principal.

226. The duties of the Principal, (who shall be responsible to the Minister of Education for the proper conduct of the Training Institute), shall be as follows:—

(*a*) Throughout the session he shall take general charge of the teachers-in-training.

(b) During the first two weeks of the session he shall take especial charge of the teachers-in-training, and shall give them such preliminary instruction as is herein provided.

(c) If himself a Department Master, he shall perform in addition such duties towards the teachers-in-training as are required from a Department Master.

(d) He shall arrange the division of duties among the members of his staff.

(e) He shall from time to time visit the class-rooms of the different members of his staff while they are in charge of the teachers-in-training, and shall satisfy himself that the design of the Training Institute is being properly carried out.

(f) At the close of the session he shall furnish the Examining Inspector, for transmission to the Minister of Education, a statement in a form to be provided, of the standing of each teacher-in-training, as shown by the Training Registers of the Department Masters and by the record of such examinations as may have been held with a view to determine the progress and qualifications of the teacher-in-training.

Duties of a Department Master.

227. Each Department Master shall be responsible to the Principal for the discharge of his duties in connection with the training of teachers, and shall be subject to his control in all matters pertaining thereto, with the right of appeal to the Minister of Education in case of dispute. He shall have charge of the teachers-in-training while taking up the subjects of his department, and shall give them such instruction as is herein provided. He shall keep a Training Register, to be provided by the Minister of Education, in which he shall record form time to time his estimate of the capacity of the teachers-in-training as evidenced by them while under his charge.

Duties of a Teacher-in-Training.

228. The teacher-in-training shall attend regularly and punctually during the whole session of the Training Institute, and shall be subject to the discipline of the Principal, with an appeal, in case of dispute, to the Minister of Education. Before attending the Training Institute, he shall make himself acquainted with the following professional text-books, as a preparation for his course of training:

(a) An Introduction to the History of Educational Theories. By Oscar Browning.

(b) School Management. By Joseph Landon.

(*c*) The Culture demanded by Modern Life.   By E. L. Youmans.

(*d*) Education.   By Herbert Spencer.

General Directions as to Management.

229. The session of each Training Institute shall consist of four sections:—

(*a*) During the first week, the Principal shall take especial charge of the teachers-in-training, as herein prescribed.

(*b*) During the next six weeks, the Department Masters shall, each in succession as follows, take especial charge of the teachers-in-training, as herein prescribed :—

(1) The first two weeks shall be devoted to the *English*   Department
(2) " third week   "   "   *Science*   "
(3) " fourth "   "   "   *Mathematical*   "
(4) " fifth   "   "   "   *Classical*   "
(5) " sixth   "   "   "   *Modern Languages* "

(*c*) The next six weeks shall be devoted by the teachers-in-training to systematic observation and practice of teaching in the different departments, under the supervision of the members of the staff, according to a weekly programme to be prepared by the Principal for each member of the staff and for each teacher-in-training.

(*d*) During the last week, the teachers-in-training shall not be required to teach, but shall review their work in preparation for the coming Examinations, with such assistance from the Training Institute staff as may be necessary.

230. When the special instruction in a department has been discontinued, illustrative teaching by the Department Master and practice in teaching by the teachers-in-training shall be continued in that department, according to the weekly programme prepared by the Principal, who shall make due allowance for the special requirements of each teacher-in-training and for the time required, during the second section of the session, for new subjects.

231. During the first week of the session the Principal shall discuss with the teachers-in-training the organization, classification, and management of a High School, with especial reference to the Collegiate Institute with which the Training Institute is connected.   He shall also give them directions as to the best methods of deriving benefit from observation and criticism of the teaching, explaining to them the course and their duties therewith.   He shall accompany them to the class-rooms on their visits of observation, and shall there illustrate the principles he has laid down.   During this period the other members of the staff shall co-operate with the Principal as he may direct.

232. During the period specially devoted to his department, the Department Master shall develop systematically the best modes of dealing with each subject in his department at each stage of a pupil's progress, using as the basis of his discussions the text-books prescribed, and illustrating his explanations by subsequent teaching.

233. Before teaching a class in presence of the teachers-in-training, the Department Master shall lay before them the purpose and plan of the lesson. He shall require them to take notes of the lesson, and shall discuss with them afterwards the observations they have made.

234. After consultation with the Principal, the Department Master shall assign to the teachers-in-training the lessons in his own department ; and, when doing so, he shall keep in view the interests of his ordinary pupils, arranging the work so as to secure both variety and progress.

235. When the teacher-in-training himself takes charge of a class, the Department Master shall leave him as much as possible to his own resources, and shall, during the progress of the lesson, take notes for subsequent entry in his Training Register. At some suitable time he shall criticise fully and freely the lesson as given by the teacher-in-training.

236. The teacher-in-training shall devote the first week of the session wholly to the preparatory course herein prescribed. During the rest of the session, besides continuing, under supervision, his daily observations, he shall each day teach, under the direction of one of the staff, at least one of the regular classes of the school, taking the different subjects and forms in rotation, and making himself especially familiar with the work of the lower forms.

237. A teacher-in-training shall not attempt to teach a lesson before the mode of dealing with the subject has been illustrated for him by the Department Master. The lesson to be taught shall be assigned to him in time to allow sufficient preparation on the part of all who are to be present, to teach it themselves or to criticise the teaching of others.

238. Before attempting to teach a lesson, the teacher-in-training shall hand to the Department Master in charge a scheme of the lesson, setting forth its purpose and plan. If necessary, this scheme shall be criticised by the Master before the teacher-in-training attempts to teach the lesson.

239. Under the supervision of the Department Master, the teachers-in-training shall teach before one another, and shall at some suitable time thereafter criticise one another's teaching in presence of the Department Master who shall direct the discussion.

240. When the teacher-in-training has acquired some skill in the management of classes, he shall occasionally be entrusted with a class, or a subdivision of a class, in a room in which no member of the staff is present. With him shall be associated another teacher-in-training, who shall afterwards, in the presence of the Department Master, criticise the method and management of his associate.

241. Teachers-in-training who desire to become teachers of special departments shall devote themselves chiefly to these departments, but every teacher-in-training shall teach all the subjects covered by his non-professional certificate as often as may be considered advisable by the Principal.

242. Candidates for First Class Public School Certificates shall take only such parts of the course as are suitable for them ; and, as far as may be necessary, they shall receive special training, subject, however, to the conditions imposed on all teachers-in-training.

243. Teachers-in-training who have no knowledge of Music, Drawing, Drill and Calisthenics, and who desire to obtain a certificate of competency in these subjects, shall study them under the Institute Masters, who shall also instruct them in the best modes of teaching these subjects. As soon as they are adjudged able to do so, they shall teach these subjects in the lower forms of the Collegiate Institute.

Examinations.

244. During the session, the teachers-in-training shall be subjected to such oral and written examinations on the course of study as the Principal may deem expedient.

245. At the close of the session, the teacher-in-training shall be subjected to an examination in Practical Teaching by one of the High School Inspectors, at the Training Institute at which he has been trained ; and also to a written examination on papers prepared by the Departmental Examiners, on the subjects hereinafter detailed.

246. At the Examination in Practical Teaching, each candidate shall be allowed to teach lessons which he has prepared for the occasion, and a scheme of which he shall hand to the examiner; but he shall also teach lessons the subjects of which shall be selected by the examiner, sufficient time, however, being allowed for preparation in this case also. The results of these examinations, together with the report of the Principal, based on the record in the Training Register, shall determine the final standing of each candidate.

247. No certificate shall be awarded to a candidate who fails to satisfy the examiners that he has made himself acquainted both theoretically and practically with the best methods of teaching at least the elements of all the subjects covered by his non-professional certificate. The professional certificate of each passed candidate shall show in detail those departments or subjects which he is most competent to teach. The Departmental Examiners shall have power to reject any candidate who may show himself deficient in scholarship.

Subjects for Final Examination.

248. The written examination at the close of each term of a Training Institute shall embrace the following subjects and text-books:—

(*a*) Mental and Moral Science in their relation to the work of teaching Observation, and the training of the Senses; Association; Memory; Reasoning; Imagination; The Conduct of the Understanding; The Will, and how to train it; Habit and Character; Authority and Discipline; Rewards and Punishment.

(*b*) The History of Education.

(*c*) The practical application of the principles of Education:—School Organization and Management; Special Methods in the Departments of *English, Mathematics, Science, Classics, French* and *German.*

(*d*) Hygiene; School-law in reference to the duties of teachers and pupils.

Text-books.

1. The History of Education.

(*a*) Introduction to the History of Educational Theories. By O. Browning.

(*b*) Systems of Education. By J. Gill.

(*c*) Lectures on the History of Education. By Jos. Payne. Or,

Essays on Educational Reformers. By R. H. Quick, M.A.

2. The Science of Education.

(*a*) Education as a Science. By Alex. Bain, LL.D.

(*b*) The Action of Examinations. By H. Latham.

3. The Principles and Practice of Teaching.

(*a*) School Management. By Joseph Landon.

(*b*) Lectures on Teaching. By J. G. Fitch, M.A.

(*c*) Teacher's Manual of Method and Organization. By Robert Robinson.

(*d*) Education. By Herbert Spencer.

(*e*) The Culture demanded by Modern Life. By E. L. Youmans.

4. Hygiene. (See Syllabus for Normal Schools.)

5. School Law. (Public and High Schools Act, 1885, and Regulations.)

MISCELLANEOUS.

Religious Instruction.

249. Every Public and High School shall be opened with the Lord's Prayer, and closed with the reading of the Scriptures and the Lord's Prayer, or the prayer sanctioned by the Department of Education.

250. The portions of Scripture used shall be taken from selections authorized for that purpose, by the Department of Education, and shall be read without comment or explanation.

251. Where a 'teacher claims to have conscientious scruples against opening and closing the school as herein provided, he shall notify the Trustees to that effect in writing.

252. No pupil shall be required to take part in the exercises above referred to against the wish of his parent or guardian, expressed in writing to the master of the school.

253. When required by the Trustees, the Ten Commandments shall be repeated at least once a week.

254. The Trustees shall place a copy of the authorized Readings in each department of the Public and High Schools under their jurisdiction, within one year from the date hereof.

255. The clergy of any denomination, or their authorized representatives, shall have the right to give religious instruction to the pupils of their own church, in each school-house at least once a week, after the hour of closing of the school in the afternoon ; and if the clergy of more than one denomination apply to give religious instruction in the same school-house, the School Board or Trustees shall decide on what day of the week the school-house shall be at the disposal of the clergyman of each denomination, at the time above stated. But it shall be lawful for the School Board or Trustees and clergyman of any denomination to agree upon any hour of the day at which a clergyman, or his authorized representative, may give religious instruction to the pupils of his own church, provided it be not during the regular hours of the school.*

GRANTS TO SCHOOLS IN NEW AND POOR TOWNSHIPS.

256. All sums of money appropriated by the Legislative Assembly in aid of schools in new and poor townships, will be distributed by the Education Department, subject to the following conditions :—

---

* The Regulations prescribing the "Hours of Daily Teaching" provide that they shall not exceed six hours in duration, but "a less number of hours of daily teaching may be determined upon in any Public School, at the option of the Trustees." Arrangement may, therefore, be made by the Trustees for closing the ordinary school work earlier than the usual hour, on certain days, so that time may be given for Religious Instruction.

(1) That a School Section with definite boundaries has been set apart by the Township Council, having jurisdiction, or, where no municipal organization exists, by the Stipendiary Magistrate, or by him and the Public School Inspector, if any, under the authority of the forty-first section of the Public Schools Act, 1885.

(2) That Trustees have been duly elected for such section.

(3) That a building and other suitable accommodation for the school, have been provided by the Trustees.

(4) That a teacher holding a valid certificate has been employed by the Trustees for at least six months of the year.

(5) That the half-yearly and yearly reports in the prescribed forms have been sent in to the Inspector, at the times specified, and certified by him as satisfactory.

(6) That the assessed value of the section and the financial condition of the ratepayers are such as to render additional aid absolutely necessary.

257. In townships with municipal organization the grant made by the Education Department shall not exceed the special grant made by the township or county, except in such cases as are reported exceptional by the Inspector.

258. Nothing in these regulations shall be construed as establishing the claim of any school upon the Poor School Fund beyond the discretion of the Education Department.

259. On the receipt of the report of the Inspector, the Minister of Education will make such recommendations to the Lieutenant-Governor, as he may deem expedient.

INDIAN SCHOOLS AND THEIR INSPECTION.

260. Every teacher in an Indian school shall have a speaking acquaintance with the Indian language, and shall, as far as possible, give his instructions in English.

261. The qualifications of teachers shall be regulated by the County or District Board of Examiners. A certificate of having passed the entrance examination prescribed for High Schools and Collegiate Institutes may be accepted in lieu of any other certificate.

262. The subjects of study in these schools shall be as follows, viz. :— Reading, Writing, Object Lessons, Elementary Drawing Elementary Arithmetic (the four simple rules), Elementary Geography (the maps of the World and Dominion of Canada), Spelling and Grammar (formation and analysis of simple sentences).

263. The County Inspector, in conjunction with the Indian Agent, shall have a controlling influence in the selection of teachers, except in the case of such schools as are established by any religious denomination under the Regulations of the Department of Indian Affairs. The Inspectors shall report upon the competency of the teacher of each Indian school inspected by him, and such other matters as may, in his opinion, affect the interests of the school.

264. A fee of six dollars ($6) per visit and legitimate travelling expenses will be paid the Inspector by the Indian Department for two visits per annum.

LIBRARIES.

265. In case of the establishment of a Township Library, the Township Council may either cause the books to be deposited in one place, or recognise each School Section within its jurisdiction as a branch of the Township Library Corporation, and cause the Library to be divided into parts or sections and allow each of these parts or sections of the Library to be circulated in succession in each School Section.

266. Each Township Library shall be under the management of the Township Corporation; and each Branch or School Section Library shall be under the management of the Board of School Trustees. The Township Council shall appoint or remove the Librarian for the Township; and each Board of Trustees shall appoint or remove the Librarian for the School Section. In default of such appointment, the teacher shall act as Librarian.

267. Each Township Council and each Board of School Trustees receiving Library Books must provide a proper case for the books, with a lock and key; and shall cause the case and books to be kept in some safe place and repaired when injured; and shall also provide sufficient wrapping paper to cover the books, and writing paper to enable the Librarian to keep minutes of the delivery and return of books, and write the needful notes or letters. The Township Council and School Trustees are responsible for the security and preservation of the books in their charge.

268. When any books are taken in charge by the Librarian, he shall make out a full and complete catalogue of them; and at the foot of each catalogue the Librarian shall sign a receipt to the following effect:

" I, A. B., do hereby acknowledge that the books specified in the preceding catalogue have been delivered to me by the Municipal Council of the Township of————, (or, as the case may be,) by the Trustees of the School Section No.————, in the Township of————, to be carefully kept by me as their Librarian, for the use of the inhabitants within their jurisdiction, according to the regulations prescribed by the authority of the Statute for the management of Public School Libraries, to be accounted for by me according to said regulations, to said Council (or Trustees as the case may be), and to be delivered to my successors in office. Dated," etc. Such catalogue, with the Librarian's receipt, having been examined by such Council or Trustees, or by some person or persons appointed by them, and found to be correct, shall be delivered to such Council or Trustees, and shall be kept among their official papers.

269. The Librarian shall be accountable to the Trustees or Council appointing him for the cost of every book that is missing, or for the whole series of which it formed a part. The Librarian shall be also accountable in like manner for any injury which a book may appear to have sustained by being soiled, defaced, torn, or otherwise injured ; and shall be relieved from such accountability only by the trustees or Council, on its being satisfactorily shown to them that some resident within their jurisdiction is chargeable for the cost of the book so missing, or for the amount of injury so done to any work.

270. The Librarian shall see that in each book belonging to the Library the number of the book and the name of the Library to which it belongs are written either on a printed label pasted inside the cover of the book, or on the first blank leaf of it; and he shall on no account give out any book which is not thus numbered and identified. He shall also cause all the books to be covered with strong wrapping paper, on the back of which is to be written the title of the book, and the number in large figures. As new books are added, the numbers shall be continued, and they shall in no case be altered ; so that if the book be lost, its number and title must be continued on the catalogue, with a note that it is missing.

271. The Librarian shall keep a blank book, which may consist of a few sheets of writing paper stitched together—ruled across the width of the paper, so as to leave five columns of the proper size, for the following entries—to be written lengthwise of the paper: In the first column, the Title and No. of the book ; in the second column, the Name and Residence of the person to whom delivered ; in the third column, Date of Delivery ; in the fourth column, the Date of its Return ; in the fifth column, Remarks respecting the condition of the books, as good, injured, torn or defaced.

272. The Librarian shall act at all times and in all things according to the orders of the Corporation appointing him ; and in case of his removal or suspension he shall deliver to his successor, or to the order of his Trustees or Council, all books, catalogues and papers appertaining or relating to the Library ; and if they are found to be satisfactory, his Trustees or Council, or successor in office, shall give him a receipt to that effect. But if any of the books shall have been lost, or in anywise injured, the Librarian shall account or pay for such loss or injury, unless released by his Trustees or Council.

273. The Trustees and Council shall attend faithfully to the interests of their Library; they shall at all times when they think proper, and as often as possible, examine the books carefully, and compare the books with the catalogue, and note such as are missing or injured ; and see that all forfeitures are promptly collected, and that injuries done to books are promptly repaired, and that the Library is properly managed and taken care of.

274. The foregoing regulations shall apply to Branch School Section Libraries, as well as to School Section Libraries; also to Township Councils, to the same extent as to Trustees of School Sections, and to Township Libraries, to the same extent as to School Section Libraries, and to the residents in a Township in which there are no School Section Libraries, to the same extent as to the residents of a School Section; likewise to the Librarian of a Township to the same extent as to a Librarian of a School Section.

275. When a Township Councillor or School Trustee shall be notified as having incurred a forfeiture for detaining, injuring, or destroying a book borrowed from the Library, he shall not act as a judge in his own case, but such case shall be decided upon by other members, or a majority of them, of the Township Council or School Corporation authorised to act in the matter. In all cases, the acts of a majority of a Corporation shall be considered as the acts of the Corporation.

276. The Council or Trustees have authority, if they shall think proper (according to the common practice of circulating libraries), to require the borrower to deposit with the Librarian a sum equal to the cost of the book taken by him, as a security for its safe return, and the payment for any injury which may be done to it.

277. These regulations shall apply to Cities, Towns, and Incorporated Villages, as well as to School Sections.

278. The Inspectors of schools shall inspect and inquire into the state and operations of the Libraries or Branch Libraries within their respective jurisdictions, and give the results of their observations and inquiries in their annual reports; and each Township and School Section Corporation shall report annually, at the time of making the annual School Reports, the condition of their Libraries, with the number of volumes in each, and the success and influence of the system.

SUPERANNUATED TEACHERS' FUND.

279. In order to be entitled to any portion of the Legislative Appropriation for Superannuated Teachers every Teacher of a High, Public or Separate School, and every Inspector, must have contributed $4 annually to the Superannuation Fund during the whole time of his professional service.

280. Arrears, if any, from 1854 inclusive, (if the applicant was then teaching,) shall be charged at the rate of $5 per annum, and must be paid before the applicant ceases teaching. All arrears must be paid before 1st July, 1886.

281. In the case of Inspectors, or Local Superintendents, who are now Inspectors, services as an Inspector shall be considered equivalent to services as a Teacher.

282. In the case of Teachers or Inspectors under sixty years of age, proof of disability must be furnished annually to the Department. The retiring allowance shall be withdrawn whenever the disability ceases, and the recipient shall annually present himself to the Inspector, in order that he may report thereon to the Minister.

283. Teachers or Inspectors, sixty years of age, are entitled to Superannuation, provided the regulations aforementioned regarding payment and arrears are complied with, without proof of disability. In all cases evidence of good moral character is required.

TEXT-BOOKS.

284. No book shall hereafter be authorized as a text-book in any Public School until the copyright thereof has been vested in the Education Department.

285. Every text-book for Public or High Schools printed and published in Canada, shall be subject, at any stage of its manufacture, to the inspection and approval of the Department in regard to printing, binding, and paper.

286. A sample copy of every edition of every authorized book shall be deposited in the Education Department by the publisher, and no edition of any book shall be considered as approved without a certificate from the Minister of Education approving thereof.

287. Every authorized book shall bear the imprint of the publisher, and shall show upon the cover or title page the authorized retail price, and no part of the book shall be used for advertising purposes, without the written consent of the Department.

288. The Education Department may require the publisher of any text-book to make such alterations from time to time as may be deemed expedient; but no alterations in contents, typography, binding, paper, or any other material respects, shall, in any case, be made without the approval of the Education Department.

289. Every publisher of an authorized text-book shall, before placing any edition of such authorized book upon the market, execute such agreements and give such security for the due fulfilment of these regulations as may be required by the Education Department.

290. All authorized text-books may be published by any firm of publishers in Ontario on the payment to the original publishers of such sum or sums of money as may be agreed upon by arbitrators to be appointed for that purpose by the publishers concerned and the Minister of Education respectively.

291. The Minister of Education may, at his discretion, after making full enquiry into the cost of manufacture, reduce the retail price of any authorized text-book. He may also remove such book from the list of authorized text-books, if the publishers fail to comply with the regulations of the Education Department, or if it be considered to be in the public interest so to do. ,

292. In case the Education Department shall at any time recommend any books as aids to the teacher, for private reference or study, it is to be distinctly understood that such books are not to be used as text-books by the pupils, and any teacher who permits such books, or any other book not authorized as a text-book for the public schools, to be used, as such shall be liable to such penalties as are imposed by the School Act.

GENERAL DIRECTIONS TO TRUSTEES.

Procedure at School Meetings.

293. The notice calling an annual or special meeting should be signed by the Secretary by direction of the trustees, or by a majority of the trustees themselves. The corporate seal need not be attached to it.

294. Any ratepayer may call the meeting to order as soon as the hour appointed arrives, and nominate a chairman

295. The business of all school meetings should be conducted according to the following rules of order :—

(1) *Addressing chairman.*—Every elector shall rise previously to speaking, and address himself to the chairman.

(2) *Order of speaking.*—When two or more electors rise at once, the chairman shall name the elector who shall speak first, when the other elector, or electors, shall next have the right to address the meeting in the order named by the chairman.

(3) *Motion to be read.*—Each elector may require the question or motion under discussion to be read for his information at any time, but not so as to interrupt an elector who may be speaking.

(4) *Speaking twice.*—No elector shall speak more than twice on the same question or amendment without leave of the meeting, except in explanation of something which may have been misunderstood, or until every one choosing to speak shall have spoken.

(5) *Protest.*—No protest against an election, or other proceedings of the school meeting, shall be received by the chairman. All protests must be sent to the inspector within twenty days at least after the meeting.

(6) *Adjournment.*—A motion to adjourn a school meeting shall always be in order, provided that no second motion to the same effect shall be made until after some intermediate proceedings shall have been had.

(7) *Motions to be in writing and seconded.*—A motion cannot be put from the chair, or debated, unless the same be seconded. If required by the chairman, all motions must be reduced to writing.

(8) *Withdrawal of a motion.*—After a motion has been announced or read by the chairman, it shall be deemed to be in possession of the meeting; but may be withdrawn at any time before decision, by the consent of the meeting.

(9) *Kind of motions to be received.*—When a motion is under debate no other motion shall be received, unless to amend it, or to postpone it, or for adjournment.

(10) *Order of putting motion.*—All questions shall be put in the order in which they move. Amendments shall all be put before the main motion; the last amendment first, and so on.

(11) *Reconsidering motion.*—A motion to reconsidsr a vote may be made by any elector at the same meeting; but no vote of reconsideration shall be taken more than once on the same question at the same meeting.

296. At the end of every annual or special meeting the Chairman should sign the minutes, and send forthwith to the Inspector a copy of the same signed by himself and the Secretary.

297. Every Trustee declared elected by the Chairman of the School Meeting is a legal Trustee until his election is set aside by proper authority.

298. The seal of the School Corporation should not be affixed to letters or notices, but only to contracts, agreements, deeds, or other papers, which are designed to bind the Trustees as a corporation for the payment of money, or the performance of any specified act, duty or thing.

Care of School Property.

299. Trustees should appoint one of their own number or some responsible person to look after petty repairs, such as fixing fences, outhouses, walks, windows, seats, blackboards, and stoves.

300. No public school house or school plot (unless otherwise provided for in the deed), or any building, furniture, or other thing pertaining thereto, shall be used or occupied for any other than Public School purposes, wtihout the express permission of the Trustees acting as a corporation.

5

301. Provision should be made by every school corporation for scrubbing and sweeping the school house regularly, for whitewashing walls and ceilings at least annually during the summer holidays, and for making fires one hour before the time for opening school, from the first of November until the first of April in each year.

Arbor Day.

302. The first Friday in May should be set apart by the Trustees of every rural school and incorporated village for the purpose of planting shade trees, making flower beds and otherwise improving and beautifying the school grounds.

Fire Drill.

303. In every school house consisting of more than one story the pupils should be regularly trained in the fire drill, in order to prevent accidents from the alarm of fire.